PORTUGUESE STUDIES

VOLUME 26 NUMBER 1
2010

The Portuguese-Speaking Diaspora in Great Britain and Ireland

Founding Editor
HELDER MACEDO

Guest Editors
JAINE BESWICK
MARK DINNEEN

Editors
FRANCISCO BETHENCOURT
RICARDO SOARES DE OLIVEIRA
JULIET PERKINS
LÚCIA SÁ
DAVID TREECE
ABDOOLKARIM VAKIL

Editorial Assistant
RICHARD CORRELL

Production Editor
GRAHAM NELSON

MODERN HUMANITIES RESEARCH ASSOCIATION

PORTUGUESE STUDIES

A biannual multi-disciplinary journal devoted to research on the cultures, societies, and history of the Lusophone world

International Advisory Board

DAVID BROOKSHAW	MARIA MANUEL LISBOA
JOÃO DE PINA CABRAL	KENNETH MAXWELL
IVO JOSÉ DE CASTRO	PAULO DE MEDEIROS
THOMAS F. EARLE	LAURA DE MELLO E SOUZA
JOHN GLEDSON	MARIA IRENE RAMALHO
ANNA KLOBUCKA	SILVIANO SANTIAGO

Articles to be considered for publication may be on any subject within the field but should not exceed 7,500 words and should be written in English. The Editorial Assistant is willing to undertake translations of texts from Portuguese if required; there will be a charge for this service. Contributions should be submitted in a form ready for publication in English and sent as an email attachment to the Editorial Assistant at richard.correll@kcl.ac.uk. The text should conform precisely to the conventions of the *MHRA Style Guide*, 2nd edn, 2008 (978-0-947623-76-0), obtainable from www.style.mhra.org.uk, price £6, US $15, €10; an online version is also available from the same address. Quotations and references should be carefully checked. Any quotations in Portuguese must be accompanied by an English translation. *Portuguese Studies* regrets that it must charge contributors with the cost of corrections in proof which the Editors in their discretion think excessive. Copies of books for review should be sent to The Reviews Editor, *Portuguese Studies*, Department of Portuguese and Brazilian Studies, King's College London, Strand, London WC2R 2LS, UK.

Copies of *Portuguese Studies* may be ordered from Subscriptions Department, Maney Publishing, Suite 1C, Joseph's Well, Hanover Walk, Leeds LS3 1AB, UK; email mhra@maney.co.uk. The journal is also available to individual members of the Modern Humanities Research Association in return for a composite membership subscription payable in advance. Further information about the activities of the MHRA and individual membership can be obtained from the Honorary Secretary, Prof. David Gillespie, School of European Studies and Modern Languages, University of Bath, Bath BA2 7AY, UK, or from the website at www.mhra.org.uk.

Parts of this work may be reproduced as permitted under legal provisions for fair dealing (or fair use) for the purposes of research, private study, criticism, or review, or when a relevant collective licensing agreement is in place. All other reproduction requires the written permission of the copyright holder who may be contacted at rights@mhra.org.uk.

ISSN 0267-5315
ISBN 978-1-907322-07-5

© 2010 THE MODERN HUMANITIES RESEARCH ASSOCIATION

Portuguese Studies vol. 26 no. 1

The Portuguese-Speaking Diaspora in Great Britain and Ireland

CONTENTS

Preface	4
Introduction JAINE BESWICK AND MARK DINNEEN	5
Portuguese Migrant Worker Experiences in Northern Ireland's Market Town Economy MARTIN EATON	10
Portuguese Migrant Workers in the UK: A Case Study of Thetford, Norfolk JOSÉ CARLOS PINA ALMEIDA AND DAVID CORKILL	27
Migrant Identities, Sociolinguistic and Sociocultural Practices: Portuguese and Spanish Migrations to the South Coast of England JAINE BESWICK AND ALICIA POZO-GUTIÉRREZ	41
A Transnational Space? Transnational Practices, Place-Based Identity and the Making of 'Home' among Brazilians in Gort, Ireland OLIVIA SHERINGHAM	60
Migrant Languages in a Multi-Ethnic Scenario: Brazilian Portuguese-Speakers in London ANA SOUZA	79
Family and Transmission: Collective Memory in Identification Practices of Madeirans on Jersey VANESSA MAR-MOLINERO	94
Nas Terras de Sua Majestade: Portuguese Emigrants to Britain in the Works of Maria Ondina Braga CLAIRE WILLIAMS	111
Abstracts	123

Preface

Portuguese structural emigration from the early fifteenth to the late twentieth century involved more than five million people, according to estimates by Vitorino Magalhães Godinho — an impressive number for a population which grew in that period of time from one to ten million. The idea of a reversal of this tendency, in the sense of Portugal becoming a country of net immigration after decolonization, in 1975, was indicated by Rui Pena Pires and Fernando Luís Machado, but this has been challenged by Maria Ioannis Baganha, who has shown a steady, though reduced, net outflow of emigration over the past decades.

By contrast, Brazil is a country built upon European immigration and the African slave trade. The abolition of the slave trade in 1850, and the final abolition of slavery in 1888, triggered a massive European immigration — the country received five million immigrants between 1820 and 1930, of which *c.* 30 per cent were Portuguese. The origins, destinations and main activities of the immigrants have been well studied by Robert Rowland, Zuleika Alvim, Altiva Pilatti Balhana and Maria Stella Ferreira Levy. However, Brazil in turn became a country of emigration in the last decades of the twentieth century, and we can now talk about a Brazilian diaspora with a visible impact on many different countries, particularly the United States, the United Kingdom, France and Portugal.

Given the time-scales, the studies of emigration are naturally more developed in the case of Portugal than of Brazil. The pioneering research by Jerry R. Williams, Maria Beatriz Rocha Trindade and Caroline Brettell has shone new light upon Portuguese emigrant communities in the United States and France, employing the methods of demography, anthropology and the political sciences. Further research has been carried out in different countries, such as Germany, but Great Britain and Ireland have not been studied at the same level, even though they have been the destination of a new generation of Portuguese and Brazilian emigrants. This is why *Portuguese Studies* immediately welcomed the suggestion by Jaine Beswick and Mark Dinneen of publishing a thematic volume on this neglected subject. We hope this excellent collection of studies, which covers a wide range of approaches (such as sociolinguistic, sociocultural, sociopolitical, socio-economic, anthropological and literary), will become a landmark, and will serve to stimulate future research.

THE EDITORS

Introduction
The Portuguese-Speaking Diaspora in Great Britain and Ireland

JAINE BESWICK AND MARK DINNEEN

Since the sixteenth century and the voyages of the discoveries, emigration has played a pivotal role in Portuguese life and culture. However, huge numbers of native Portuguese speakers from Brazil, Angola, Mozambique, Guinea Bissau, Cape Verde, Macau, São Tomé and Príncipe, and East Timor have also shared such migratory experiences across the globe, and have thus helped to establish important Portuguese-speaking diasporas throughout Europe, the Americas and beyond. There has been a upsurge of interest in diaspora studies in the last twenty-five years or so, but it is somewhat surprising that despite the plethora of research carried out into the phenomenon of Portuguese-speaking migrations to Canada and the USA from the Azores and Brazil,[1] and to other countries in Europe,[2] Portuguese-speaking migrations to Great Britain and Ireland have not featured more prominently. This special issue of *Portuguese Studies* examines just a few examples of Portuguese-speaking migration to Great Britain and Ireland, but each case study is highly significant and their inclusion here goes a long way to rectifying this glaring omission from diaspora studies. Building on two informal workshops held at Manchester Metropolitan University in 2007 and at the University of Southampton in 2008, it represents the first compilation of leading

---

[1] Amongst the most significant work on migration to New England is the literary production of Onésimo T. Almeida, himself an Azorean migrant. See also Carmen Ramos, *The Metaphorical 'Tenth Island' in Azorean Literature: The Theme of Emigration in the Azorean Imagination* (Lampeter: Edwin Mellen Press, 2006). Recent non-literary work includes Domingos Marques and Manuela Marujo, *With Hardened Hands: A Pictorial History of Portuguese Immigration to Canada in the 1950s* (Toronto: New Leaf Publications, 1993); *The Portuguese in Canada: From the Sea to the City*, ed. by José Carlos Teixeira and Victor M. P. da Rosa (Toronto: University of Toronto Press, 2000). For an interesting overview of Azorean and Cape Verde migration to the US, see David E. Bertão, *The Portuguese Shore Whalers of California, 1854–1904* (San Jose: Portuguese Heritage Publications of California, 2006); for Brazilian migration see for example Maxine L. Margolis, *An Invisible Minority: Brazilians in New York City* (Boston, MA: Allyn and Bacon, 1998). Andrea Klimt's early work looked at Portuguese migration to Germany, but her latest work revisits migration to the US: Kimberly da Costa Holton and Andrea Klimt, *Community, Culture and the Makings of Identity: Portuguese-Americans Along the Eastern Seaboard* (Dartmouth: University of Massachusetts Dartmouth, Center for Portuguese Studies and Culture, 2009).

[2] In Europe, the most prominent recent work is that of Michèle Koven, *Selves in Two Languages: Bilinguals' Verbal Enactments of Identity in French and Portuguese* (Amsterdam and Philadelphia: John Benjamins, 2007).

interdisciplinary investigation of these particular diasporic groups, and seeks to shed light on their migratory patterns, their particular migrant experiences and issues, as well as their transnational and cross-cultural relationships.

Within the Portuguese-speaking diaspora in the British Isles there are many migrants who harbour plans to return to the homeland as soon as they have amassed enough savings to provide lasting financial security. However, many end up settling in the receptor society on a long-term or even permanent basis. The social, cultural and linguistic impact they frequently exert on the local space and the vital role they can come to play in the local economy are clearly illustrated in some of the essays in this collection. The research involved is certainly long overdue. At the same time that public debate on immigration is intensifying more than ever, with increasing concern being expressed in the media over such issues as social exclusion, racism and cultural conflict, academic research on diaspora continues apace. Broadly, contemporary studies have taken one of two directions: theoretical advancement,[3] or specific case studies.[4] Further, the recent UK-based and AHRC-funded research programme titled 'Diasporas, Migration and Identities', has carried out groundbreaking research into global diaspora and migration, whilst conferences such as that held in Lisbon in 2008 titled 'Narrating the Portuguese Diaspora Conference: International Conference on Storytelling', serve to bring together academics with an interest in Lusophone postcolonial studies. To date, however, with the notable exception of earlier work by authors contributing to this issue,[5] the study of the Portuguese-speaking diaspora in Britain and Ireland has largely been neglected both in public and academic discourse.[6]

---

[3] Recent work includes *Theorising Diaspora: A Reader*, ed. by Jana Evans Braziel and Anita Manur (Malden, MA: Blackwell, 2003) and Robin Cohen, *Global Diasporas: An Introduction* (London: UCL Press, 1997). For the latest overview of theoretical constructs and intersections pertaining to diaspora, see the edited volume *Diasporas: Concepts, Identities, Intersections*, ed. by Kim Knott and Sean McLoughlin (forthcoming 2010).

[4] See for example, Michael Clyne, *Dynamics of Language Contact: English and Immigrant Languages* (Cambridge: Cambridge University Press, 2003); *The South Asian Diaspora: Transnational Networks and Changing Identities*, ed. by Rajesh Rai and Peter Reeves (Oxford: Taylor & Francis, 2008).

[5] Already published are: José Carlos Pina Almeida, 'Citizens of the World: Migration and Citizenship of the Portuguese in the UK', *Portuguese Studies*, 23, 2 (2007), 208–29; Jaine Beswick, 'The Portuguese Diaspora in Jersey', in *The Consequences of Mobility: Linguistic and Sociocultural Contact Zones*, ed. by Bent Preisler, Anne Fabricius, Harmut Haberland, Susanne Kjaerbeck and Karen Risager (Roskilde, Denmark: Roskilde University Press, 2005), online at: <http://www.ruc.dk/cuid/publikationer/publikationer/mobility/mobility2/Beswick/> [accessed 30 November 2009]; Martin Eaton, 'From Porto to Portadown: Portuguese Workers in Northern Ireland's Labour Market', *Portuguese Journal of Social Science*, 6, 3 (2008).

[6] Two exceptions from academia are: Guida Abreu, Teresa Silva and Hannah Lambert, *Portuguese Children in British Schools: England and the Channel Islands* (Luton: University of Luton, Department of Psychology, 2001) and Yara Evans, Jane Wills, Kavita Datta, Joanna Herbert, Cathy McIlwaine, Jon May, Father José Osvaldo de Araújo, Ana Carla França and Ana Paula França, *Brazilians in London: A Report for the Strangers into Citizens Campaign* (London: Queen Mary, University of London, Department of Geography, 2007).

The theorization of the concept of modern diaspora has advanced rapidly in a relatively short period of time. The pioneering work produced in the late 1980s and early 1990s tended to portray migrants as victims of circumstance, displaced through migration and exile from the homeland yet struggling against prejudice and marginalization in the receptor society.[7] Diasporas were perceived to be essentially homogeneous: shared ethnicities, memories, histories, myths of the homeland and language were seen as the cohesive forces that would support migrants within the diaspora until their projected return to the homeland. In contrast, more recent conceptualizations have emphasized the complex, heterogeneous and hybrid nature of diaspora,[8] seeing them as dynamic and proactive, not simply constantly looking back to the past in order to sustain themselves, but confronting the present and future by developing new strategies and practices in order to establish a new sense of place, belonging and role across generations. The perception of an essentially antagonistic relationship between the diaspora and the receptor country, shared by many early theorists, has largely been replaced by an emphasis on dynamic, positive interaction.

In contrast to old assumptions about the defining nature of displacement, separation and rootlessness, contemporary diaspora are increasingly seen as located at the crossroads of diverse transnational links and flows. Irrespective of geographical and territorial constraints, the globalized movement of people is creating transnational spaces in which migrants negotiate a new level of adaptation to receptor societies and, simultaneously, the continued maintenance of relations with the home country.[9] Whereas diaspora were once largely regarded as subgroups of the national population — Portuguese, Brazilian, and Angolan — it is now their transnational character in terms of linkages, practices and experience which is likely to be emphasized. More than a shared cultural identity rooted in the past, relying heavily on a repository of traditions, customs and myths, what is now stressed is how diversity and difference within a diaspora stimulates change, with identities constantly being created, recreated and redefined.

The essays in this special issue highlight the interdisciplinary nature of diaspora studies. The authors are from a wide-range of fields — linguistics, geography, sociopolitical studies, economics, and literary and cultural studies — and, unsurprisingly, they employ different theoretical approaches in their research. Although there are some striking contrasts between the groups that they examine, there are also some notable similarities; recurring themes and issues, such as migrant identity construction and the importance of language within diaspora, as well as the many issues related to the experience of settlement and integration, serve to provide strong, coherent and cohesive links between each of the essays.

[7] See for example William Safran, 'Diasporas in Modern Societies: Myths of Homeland and Return', *Diaspora*, 1, 1 (1991), 83–99.

[8] An early example is Stuart Hall, 'Cultural Identity and Diaspora', in Braziel and Manur, eds, *Theorising Diaspora*, pp. 233–46.

[9] See for example Thomas Faist, 'The Border-Crossing Expansion of Social Space: Concepts, Questions and Topics', in *Transnational Social Spaces: Agents, Networks and Institutions*, ed. by Thomas Faist and Eyüp Özveren (Aldershot: Ashgate, 2004), pp. 1–34.

Martin Eaton's essay begins by reviewing data pertaining to Portuguese migrant flows to Great Britain and Ireland, and thereby provides the context for a large part of the research represented in this special issue. However, his primary focus is the formation of spatial concentrations of Portuguese-speaking itinerant migrant workers in some relatively isolated areas of Northern Ireland, and the experiences of these migrants regarding acceptance, social integration, economic opportunities and exploitation in the workplace. Eaton shows how, despite the acute difficulties they have frequently faced, these migrants continue to provide vital labour to key areas of the Northern Irish economy.

The essay by **José Almeida** and **David Corkill** also takes an essentially socio-economic perspective, analysing employment patterns and settlement trends of ethnically diverse, multinational Portuguese-speaking migrants, particularly the well-established and highly visible diaspora based in Thetford, Norfolk. In particular, it discusses the motivations for migration and the recruitment process in Portugal, and how these impact on adaptation to the labour market, integration within the receptor society and intra-community relations. It too refers to the problems faced by the migrant workers, not least the reduction of work opportunities resulting from increasing numbers of Eastern European immigrants, but ends by emphasizing the factors that encourage many of the Portuguese-speaking families to stay in the region long-term.

A clear interdisciplinary perspective is evident in the essay by **Jaine Beswick** and **Alicia Pozo-Gutiérrez**, which primarily discusses sociolinguistic and socio-political aspects of migration. Its comparative approach offers a detailed examination of the migratory processes of the Portuguese in Bournemouth compared with Spanish groups, and discusses issues regarding sociocultural, socio-economic and sociolinguistic visibility within the receptor society. Like Almeida and Corkill's essay, it considers motivations for migration by mapping out the socio-political and socio-economic contexts of arrival, and asks whether such contexts influence linguistic, social and cultural practices, identification strategies, transnational relationships and the formation of 'community'.

Olivia Sheringham's essay makes a more detailed analysis of transnationalism as a phenomenon of global migration shift. Her study examines the recent migration experiences of a highly visible group of Brazilian migrants in a small Irish town, Gort. Again, the focus is on spatial concentrations and the formation of 'community'; here, however, the author unravels the complex relationships that these migrants are beginning to develop between their home nation and the receptor society. In particular, she emphasizes the role played by such transnational practices, arguing that the 'transnational social space' created by the Gort Brazilians not only helps them to maintain ties with the home country but also to develop a sense of local attachment.

Brazilians living in London are the focus of **Ana Souza**'s essay. This is the result of a small-scale study of the role of language in the construction of identities by a group of Brazilian mothers and their children, with reference to a range of theoretical work on social identity and language acquisition. Sousa demonstrates that the mothers' self-identity is multiple, changing according to context, and in turn how that process impacts upon their children's sense of ethnicity.

Vanessa Mar-Molinero's essay examines Jersey's relatively large and highly visible Portuguese (mostly Madeiran) diaspora, served by a firmly established infrastructure and having a significant impact on island life at all levels. She offers an intergenerational account of identity (re)construction in children of Madeiran migrants. Drawing on theories of collective memory, her research highlights the key role of the family in identity transmission, but also the sense of ambiguity and insecurity that young people often experience as a result, since they do not feel fully 'accepted' in either Madeira or Jersey.

The interviews that are central to a large part of the research represented here are at the very least an important incipient record of the experience and perceptions of the Portuguese-speaking diaspora in Britain, but relatively few members of the migrant groups involved have written accounts of their own experiences. One of the few to do just this in the twentieth century was Maria Ondina Braga, the subject of **Claire Williams**' essay. Braga, originally from the city of the same name in Portugal, lived in England in the 1950s and described her experience and mixed emotions in memoirs and fiction. Unlike most of the migrants in this study, she did not migrate for economic reasons but as an educational investment, for the experience enabled her to become a teacher of English and a translator in later life, and to acquire linguistic skills that facilitated other travels. As Williams concludes, it will be interesting to see if in the future more written accounts emerge from the expanding Portuguese-speaking diaspora of the British Isles.

What becomes clear from all the essays included in this special issue is how Great Britain and Ireland have become increasingly important destinations for Portuguese-speaking migrants over recent decades. In many large cities, in medium-sized towns and even in small market towns their presence is now highly visible, and we are at least beginning to understand the contribution they make to local economic, social and cultural life, as well as the often complex challenges they confront. These essays can only offer a snapshot of the mixed experiences, tendencies and increasingly complex relationships evident within the Portuguese-speaking diaspora in the British Isles, but we hope that collectively they make a significant contribution to furthering the understanding of some of the groups that comprise it. Above all, we hope that in some small way it can serve to encourage further research in this area, particularly through the establishment of an international research network which can extend the work to the global Portuguese-speaking diaspora.

We would like to conclude by expressing our heartfelt thanks to all those who have made this special issue possible: the authors, the editorial team of *Portuguese Studies*, and, in particular, the many informants from the various studies, who patiently and openly recounted their migrant experiences and offered their opinions and perceptions of life as migrants.

UNIVERSITY OF SOUTHAMPTON

Portuguese Migrant Worker Experiences in Northern Ireland's Market Town Economy

MARTIN EATON

Introduction

In the summer of 2008, as the Portuguese soccer team enjoyed success at the European Football Championship, residents of the small provincial town of Portadown in Northern Ireland (NI) gathered to cheer them on. In a display of inter-community co-operation, both locals and migrant workers congregated in public houses. They came together in their support for a team that carried the hopes of two small, semi-peripheral, part-industrialized countries located on the fringes of the European Union (EU). It was a union inspired, in part, by their mutual rivalry with the England football team, but also demonstrated some of the progress that has been made in integrating Portuguese workers into Northern Irish society.

The Portuguese in this part of Ulster represent a small proportion of a Portuguese emigrant community numbering at least 4.5 million worldwide.[1] This global mobilization was originally based upon exploration, colonization and, more recently, economic migration to seek a better life. Migrant outflows have tailed off since the peak period of the early 1970s, when hundreds of thousands fled from authoritarian Portugal. Nevertheless, there has been a post-millennium resurgence in emigration, induced by domestic recession, and emigration continues to be a fundamental factor shaping Portugal's sociodemographic evolution. In turn, the United Kingdom has emerged as an important destination, with Lusitanian immigrants now estimated to number anywhere between 110,000 and 250,000. While their nuclei are focused upon London and the British protectorate of the Channel Islands, there have been significant influxes into more peripheral, semi-rural regions. These secondary flows have included East Anglia, Humberside, north-west England, Wales, the Scottish borders and Northern Ireland.

With this background in mind, this article presents a brief overview of the Portuguese emigrant flows towards the United Kingdom. Our emphasis is on migrant workers, defined as: 'someone from outside the UK and Ireland who is here to seek or take up work'.[2] The study reviews a growing secondary

---

[1] Jorge C. Arroteia, 'As Comunidades Portuguesas no Mundo', *Janus* (2001), online at <www.janusonline.pt/sociedade_cultura/sociedade_2001_3_2_1_c.html> [accessed 13 Nov. 2009].

[2] Department for Employment and Learning Northern Ireland (DELNI), *A Migrant Workers Strategy for Northern Ireland* (Belfast: DELNI, 2008), p. 5.

theoretical literature and relevant statistical data before utilizing qualitative empirical research. Here, we focus upon the experiences of Portuguese-speaking migrant workers, together with the views of interested third parties, related local employers, and emergent support workers and organizations. Our spatial arena is the Northern Ireland labour market, where many migrants have been recruited by employment agencies to work in the region's agricultural harvesting, food packing, fish processing and meat packaging sectors. These businesses, in turn, are located in small market towns often distant from the region's main population centres. While the numbers of foreigners found in Northern Ireland are relatively small, many Portuguese — along with recent influxes of central- and east-European (CEE) workers — have flocked together in expressions of human gregariousness and of shared personal interests aimed at economic betterment. These spatial concentrations have had important consequences, bringing benefits to local economies, but also leading to problems in employment and socialization processes. As a result, labour market issues relating to the workers' behaviour, including the phenomena of personal 'trade-off' and exploitation, will be discussed, together with a determination of what the future might hold for these itinerant workers and their families.

Migrant Workers and Labour Markets

The majority of contemporary Portuguese migrants have been labelled as neo-classical labourers, perpetually moving in order to find jobs, to secure salaries and to remit their savings to their families at home.[3] This pattern, however, has become more complicated since the emigrants have been further motivated to travel abroad and find a better level of remuneration and more secure conditions of employment in their chosen destination countries. In relative terms, therefore, workers availed of more advantageous labour market conditions to the ones they may have been used to in their country of origin or left behind in their previous destination society, and this is now a key factor influencing their decision-making, and in turn, their exodus.

While this movement was normally the result of an individual decision, in more recent years some Portuguese emigrants have become part of a collective labour market scheme. Employment agencies, designed to engage migrant workers for the benefit of specific sectors of industry, have been set up and these have proliferated, with recruitment branches being established in country of origin and country of destination. The agents have actively sought out candidates either from lower cost/lower wage areas (such as Portugal), or from employment in similar sectors of industry (in north-west Europe) and relocated them to semi-

---

[3] Stephen Castles, 'International Migration at the Beginning of the Twenty-First Century: Global Trends and Issues', *International Social Science Journal*, 165 (2000), 269–81; Stephen Castles, 'Migration and Community Formation under Conditions of Globalisation', *International Migration Review*, 36, 4 (2002), 1143–68.

peripheral areas of the European Union (such as Northern Ireland). In so doing, they have brought new issues into the labour market, and concerns which are based, in part, upon the perception of migrant labourers replacing the indigenous workers. This idea that the immigrants 'are taking over jobs, which should be for local workers' (the 'TOJ' syndrome) is a prejudiced but very real concern in many advanced industrialized countries.[4] Here, immigration is often near the top of the political agenda, and often symptomatic of countries that may be uncertain of their national identity.[5] As a result, strains on social and economic integration into local job markets have emerged and become a contentious issue for state governance, public organizations and private agencies. In a Northern Irish context this issue was further complicated by a recent history of conflict ('the troubles') between its divided nationalist and unionist communities and their spatial boundaries. Indeed, the process of Portuguese immigration into Northern Island is unique, and integration into the local labour market is, at least at first appearances, a distant prospect.[6]

Given that little research has been carried out into these job markets, this present contribution becomes an important if tentative starting point. It is an issue deserving of attention from demographers, geographers, politicians and social commentators interested in determining the impact of relatively large numbers of a particular type of migrant worker. Initially, these were averagely educated, relatively transient, single young people seeking work and financial remuneration at a level that would be impossible to achieve in an equivalent type of job in Portugal.[7] As we will see, this initial pattern has evolved into a more widespread redistribution of workers, together with their partners and children. As such, the theoretical and practical implications for societies in both the country of origin, and of destination, should not be underestimated.

Portuguese Population Mobility

Since the start of 2000, almost 100,000 Portuguese (approximately 1 per cent of the total domestic population) have left their country of origin.[8] Many have been forced to leave as a result of home labour market difficulties,[9] including growing unemployment, fewer job opportunities, higher interest rates, the rising

[4] Bernadette C. Hayes and Lizanne Dowds, 'Social Contact, Cultural Marginality or Economic Self-Interest? Attitudes towards Immigrants in Northern Ireland', *Journal of Ethnic and Migration Studies*, 32, 3 (2006), 455–76.

[5] Sarah Spencer, 'The Challenges of Integration for the EU', *Migration Information Source* (2003) <http://www.migrationinformation.org/Feature/display.cfm?ID=170> [accessed 11 November 2009].

[6] Vani K. Borooah and John Mangan, 'Love Thy Neighbour: How Much Bigotry Is There In Western Countries?' *Kyklos*, 60, 3 (2007), 295–318.

[7] Anthony Soares, *Relatório Sobre Trabalhadores Portugueses na Irlanda do Norte* (Belfast: Multi-Cultural Resource Centre, 2002).

[8] Instituto Nacional de Estatística, *Estatísticas Demográficas* (Lisbon: INE, 2000–03).

[9] José Carlos Marques, 'E Continuam a Partir: As Migrações Portuguesas Contemporâneas', *Ler História*, 56 (2009), 27–44 (p. 41).

cost of living, increases in income and value added taxes, wage freezes, and other austerity measures imposed by successive governments.[10] A further motivating factor was that wage levels in Portugal were sometimes only a third of those in more advanced European economies, while domestically the cost of living caught up with the EU average.[11] Many working-class Portuguese found themselves caught out by this divergence of costs and earnings, which made it increasingly difficult for them to sustain a livelihood in their own country.

Between 2000 and 2003 around 83,000 (86 per cent) of Portuguese emigrants continued to follow the established route by migrating to central north-western Europe.[12] Switzerland and France remained the principal destinations,[13] but the United Kingdom had come to account for one in ten of all emigrants. Indeed, the UK outstripped Germany,[14] Spain and Luxembourg as a main receiver of Portuguese migrants. In overall terms, 73 per cent of emigrants were classified as temporary (less than one year), short term or seasonal migrants. However, in the British case, the ratio was significantly different, with 43 per cent being labelled as long term or permanently settling emigrants (more than one year). During this period almost 10,000 migrants were recorded as having travelled to the UK and the annual rate of outward movement was accelerating. It was clear that Britain was gaining significantly in its attraction. Nevertheless, it was impossible to derive an accurate total, not least because Portuguese citizens are allowed to circulate freely around the EU. Almeida has recognized the usefulness of the British Labour Force Survey,[15] which in 2005 suggested that there were 85,000 Portuguese citizens living in the UK, although some commentators believed there to be nearly 110,000 Portuguese residents at that time.[16] According to the Portuguese Consulate General (PCG) in London the real figure (given that registration was a voluntary activity) could be more than twice as high, at around a quarter of a million.[17] While most of these immigrants were located

---

[10] Economist Intelligence Unit, *Country Profile 2004 Portugal* (London: EIU, 2004).

[11] Hervé Dieux, 'Sleepwalkers of Portugal', *Le Monde Diplomatique*, August 2002, p. 2. Online at <http://mondediplo.com/2002/08/07Portugal> [accessed 11 November 2009].

[12] José Carlos Marques, 'A Emigração Portuguesa para a Europa: Desenvolvimentos Recentes', *Janus* (2001), online at <www.janusonline.pt/sociedade_cultura/sociedade_2001_3_2_6_c.html> [accessed 13 November 2009].

[13] Jorge P. Branco, 'A Comunidade Portuguesa em França (I)', *Janus* (2001), online at <www.janusonline.pt/sociedade_cultura/sociedade_2001_3_2_7_c.html> [accessed 13 November 2009].

[14] Thomas Bauer, Pedro T. Pereira, Michael Vogler and Klaus F. Zimmermann, 'Portuguese Migrants in the German Labour Market: Selection and Performance', *International Migration Review*, 36, 2 (2002), 467–91.

[15] José Carlos P. Almeida, 'Citizens of the World: Migration and Citizenship of the Portuguese in the UK', *Portuguese Studies*, 23, 2 (2007), 208–29 (p. 214).

[16] British Broadcasting Corporation, 'Portuguese Community Develops', *BBC News* (2004), online at <http://www.bbc.co.uk/guernsey/content/articles/2004/07/09/portuguese-community> [accessed 12 May 2005].

[17] Almeida, p. 220.

in the Channel Islands and London,[18] in recent years there has been spatial dispersal of the Portuguese towards more peripheral regions of Britain. Trails have developed, for example, towards East Anglia and Humberside to help in agricultural harvesting,[19] and towards north-west England (particularly around Manchester), where the Portuguese worked mainly in food production factories. Even more recently, workers have begun gravitating towards Wales, the Scottish borders and Northern Ireland.[20]

Portuguese Migrants in Northern Ireland

Northern Ireland's foreign population is dominated by communities of Chinese (estimated at 7–8000 individuals), Indian (1500), and African (1600) origin.[21] Since 2004 (and partly as a response to EU accession), CEE immigrants have proliferated, with significant numbers travelling from Lithuania, Slovakia, Russia and, in particular, from Poland.[22] Given the paucity of information on the region's foreign population and the failure of the Northern Ireland Census 2001 to delve beyond generic ethnic minority groupings, accurate migration data was once again difficult to obtain. Nevertheless, as part of a provincial population of almost 1.7 million, it was clear that foreigners remained a small but rapidly growing and increasingly diverse sector. Conservative estimates, in the early part of the decade, placed the region's Portuguese-speaking population somewhere between 700 and 1000 individuals.[23] In turn, most were Portuguese nationals with a small minority (of 10 per cent) being Portuguese-speaking individuals from associated countries such as Angola, Brazil, Mozambique and East Timor.[24] Data relating to applications for National Insurance Numbers showed that between 2003 and 2008 a total of 3618 Portuguese were registered either to work, or to

---

[18] Leo Benedictus, 'Every Race, Colour, Nation and Religion on Earth — Part Three', *Guardian Unlimited*, Friday 21 January (2005), online at <http://www.guardian.co.uk/uk/2005/jan/21/race.britishidentity/print> [accessed 11 November 2009]; Jaine Beswick, 'The Portuguese Diaspora in Jersey', in *The Consequences of Mobility*, ed. by Bent Preisler et al. (Roskilde: Roskilde University, 2005), pp. 93–105.

[19] Cindi John, 'Woes of Boston's Gang Workers', *BBC News UK* (2003), online at <http://news.bbc.co.uk/1/hi/uk/3223560.stm> [accessed 11 November 2009].

[20] David Corkill and José Carlos P. Almeida, 'The 3 P's: Portuguese Migrant Labour in East Anglia', paper to conference on the Portuguese-Speaking Diaspora in the UK, Manchester Metropolitan University, 28 June 2007.

[21] Multi-Cultural Resource Centre, *Estimated Populations of Minority Ethnic Communities in Northern Ireland* (Belfast: MCRC, 2002).

[22] South Tyrone Empowerment Programme, 'Linguistic Diversity in Dungannon' (2006), online at <http://www.communityni.org/news/linguistic-diversity-dungannon> [accessed 11 November 2009]; Naomi Pollard, Maria Latorre and Dhananjayan Sriskandarajah, *Floodgates or Turnstiles? Post-EU Enlargement Migration Flows to (and from) the UK* (London: Institute for Public Policy Research, 2008).

[23] MCRC (2002); Daniel Holder, *In Other Words? Mapping Minority Ethnic Languages in Northern Ireland* (Belfast: Multi-Cultural Resource Centre, 2003), p. 74.

[24] Soares, pp. 4–5.

claim benefits and tax credits with the region's Social Security Agency.[25] Given that the mobilization was a very recent phenomenon and the situation constantly changing, as well as there being no compulsion to register (or de-register) with the PCG, then the true figure for Portuguese immigration was perhaps higher still. The question marks surrounding these figures reflected the weak statistical hold of government agencies and the unrecorded migratory flows associated with EU freedom of movement, both into and out of the province. Nevertheless, it was clear that the Portuguese represented a minor grouping within a small foreign population in Northern Ireland.

In spatial terms, it is notable that the Portuguese were found in small but highly concentrated clusters in the new/market towns of mid-Ulster. These included Portadown and Craigavon (each conservatively estimated to contain around 200 Portuguese nationals), and the primary focus of Portuguese immigration, Dungannon (estimated at 300).[26] More recently, Portuguese workers have been drawn into the smaller outlying market towns of Antrim, Armagh, Ballymena, Ballymoney, Banbridge, Coalisland, Coleraine, Cookstown, Enniskillen, Kilkeel, Limavady, Magherafelt, Omagh, Newtownards and Rathfriland.[27] What was unusual about this distribution was that the main population centres of Belfast, Lisburn and Londonderry/Derry were largely ignored by Portuguese emigrants. This was because migrant workers were responding to changes in the rural economy, filling an 'unmet demand for low-paid labour'.[28] In effect, they were substituting themselves into the local, agriculturally based labour markets of Ulster. Here, myriad activities including fruit and vegetable harvesting, mushroom picking, sandwich making, potato, pig and poultry packing, fish processing and dairy farming have remained important. Indeed, Northern Ireland's food processing industry was the third largest manufacturing sector in the region, employing 19,000 workers and producing £2.5 billion worth of sales in 2005.[29] Much of the produce was exported and this value-added trade accounted for 'almost two-thirds of the food processing sector's output',[30] thus helping to maintain its position as a staple regional industry alongside tourism, financial services, and electronics manufacturing.

---

[25] Department for Social Development Northern Ireland, *National Insurance Number (NiNo) Applications by Nationality (April 2003–March 2008)* (Belfast: NISRA, 2008).
[26] Lisa McGreevy and Peter Bayne, 'Portuguese Pouring into Dungannon', *Tyrone Courier*, 5 September 2001, online at <http://www.ulsternetni.co.uk/cour3601/cpages/CMAIN.htm> [accessed 16 August 2005].
[27] Northern Ireland Statistical Research Agency, *Components of Population Change by Administrative Area, 2004 to 2005* (Belfast: NISRA, 2006); NISRA, *Components of Change, by Local Government District (July 2006–June 2007)* (Belfast: NISRA, 2008).
[28] Trade Union Congress, *Migrant Workers are Propping Up Rural and Small Town Britain* (London: TUC, 2004), p. 2.
[29] Anon., 'Economy Minister Praises Kerry Group', *Northern Irish News* (2007), online at <www.4ni.co.uk/northern_ireland_news.asp?id=62823> [accessed 11 November 2009].
[30] Office of the First Minister and Deputy First Minister, *Northern Ireland: Take a Closer Look* (Belfast: OFMDFM, 2004).

Portuguese Workers' Impacts

Because of the sensitivity associated with this topic area, language constraints and the levels of suspicion now surrounding the role of recruitment agencies, as well as alleged interference on the part of supervisors, it proved impossible to conduct a quantitative inquiry aimed at the Portuguese workers. However, to counteract these difficulties and begin exploring the experiences of these labour migrants, a series of in-depth, semi-structured discussions was held with representatives closely associated with the Portuguese working in Northern Ireland. These respondents included a female migrant worker from Lisbon (A), a local supermarket line manager (B), two food processing factory production managers (C & D), a local community/church worker (E), the managing director (F) and manager (G) of a sandwich-making factory, a Brazilian-born, male migrant worker (H), a support worker for Portuguese families (I), a local newspaper editor (J) and a former labour recruitment agent (K). Our informants were carefully selected as possessing knowledge of the labour market issues relating specifically to migrants in two of the main mid-Ulster market town destinations, namely Portadown and Dungannon. This important and detailed qualitative information was collected in the spring of 2006 and focused upon the segmentation of the local labour market, the problems and benefits emerging, collective societal responses, as well as the integration process undertaken by migrant workers and local communities alike. We should, of course, be aware that the empirical base was narrow and opinions put forward were value-laden. Nevertheless, field workers reported constructive discussions; quality and integrity of responses were high, and this allowed for an initial understanding and the making of tentative observations.

Our discussions confirmed, for example, that at the micro scale the influx of Portuguese workers into Northern Ireland has been both rapid and a very recent phenomenon. At first it was an individual activity but this has evolved to include a measure of family transferral into the region. (E) gave an indication of the migrant timeline whereby:

> The first group of people to come were the Portuguese appearing here in 2000. At the start it was all males arriving, most of which were aged between 20 and 30. In the last few years [however] there have been many families and middle-aged people coming to live and work here.

Our investigation showed that Portugal's immigrant community was a small and largely hidden group at the regional level, whose relative 'invisibility' was based upon their inherent desire not to draw attention to themselves. While their numbers were the subject of debate it was quite likely that current estimates (from NI records — see note 25) of up to 3600 Portuguese immigrants were conservative. Taking account of unrecorded immigration and family reconciliation the real figure was likely to be much higher, 'between 5000 and 6000 individuals' (reflecting speculation on the part of community worker E).

In spite of this uncertainty, many Portuguese immigrants have become part of a distinctive labour market where the immigrant's importance was repeatedly stressed. Indeed, without the migrant labourers, it was likely the meat processing factories (and, in turn, the rural agricultural economy) in many parts of the region would struggle to survive. As a result, prominent meat processing factories such as Moy Park, Dunbia and the O'Kane Group could have their lucrative positions in Northern Ireland's top twenty-seven companies jeopardized.[31] (C), for example, was unequivocal on this topic:

> Local people don't want to work in this [chicken processing plant] environment [...] we can't get local people to do the work so if it weren't for foreign workers the company would not be able to operate. We have such high productivity and market demand that if we failed to meet it, the factory would close down and all of us (local and migrant workers, alike) would be out of jobs.

The inherent flexibility and ready compliance afforded by the migrant worker (in comparison to a local employee), and the relatively low skill requirements of the work, also lay at the heart of the business decision to take on foreign nationals. The use of such labour was particularly relevant in these sectors, which were associated with major seasonal fluctuations, and the generally long, hard and unsocial hours that went with 'continental'-style twelve-hour shift-working patterns. To this end, (G) attested that:

> The food industry has unpredictable hours at best [...] [this factory] starts at seven and does not finish until production has stopped. For local workers with families to support, this is not seen as an acceptable condition. However, it is perfect for foreign nationals who [...] have no families to support in the immediate area.

(D) argued:

> The migrants have been able to work overtime in the past when it was not wanted [by the local workers], for instance, at Christmas and New Year holidays.

This demand-led argument meant that the employers were generally happy to have developed their supply relationships with the labour agencies[32] and were, therefore, reluctant to intervene to make agents change their ways or regulate their activities. Indeed, the factories had garnered the fruits of a well-motivated, highly productive and relatively docile immigrant labour force; one that was easily recruited (by a third party) and praised for its intrinsic work ethic. This positive image was reiterated by (F), who said that his factory had been able 'to use a large population of [Portuguese] workers keen to work at any time, any holiday to maximum effect', while (B) affirmed that 'we have (Portuguese) agency workers who come in to do shifts we have trouble filling at night'.

[31] Bank of Scotland Ireland, '*Northern Ireland's Top 100 Companies*' (Belfast: BSI, 2009).
[32] Barbara Cains, 'Managing a Non-National Workforce: Employer's Perspectives', in Equality Commission for Northern Ireland, *Employing Migrant Workers in Northern Ireland* (Belfast: ECNI, 2004), p. 5.

The role of the labour agents and the agencies they represented was very strong and it often extended from pre-arrival through to their initial travel and subsequent settlement in Northern Ireland. (A)'s narrative appeared typical of many and explained that:

> I had to give [name of employment agency] a cheque for £250 in order to secure my plane ticket [...]. On arrival, [the agency] had organized accommodation for us but it was rough with no heating, oil, electric and very little furnishing [...]. Other houses [of fellow migrant workers] were extremely poor quality, smelly [...] and some can be quite cramped.

A synthesis of information supplied by the interviewees and (K), in particular, showed that these employment agencies were both internationally and locally owned. Several were based in Porto (Portugal), and a number of others in the island of Ireland (in Belfast and Dublin). A typical agency attracted workers to factories across Northern Ireland through adverts placed in Portuguese tabloid newspapers (e.g. *Correio de Manhã*).[33] The agency would then interview potential workers and complete medical checks before signing them up and flying them to Belfast. Once in the region, they were accommodated in shared lodgings with several other agency employees and then assigned and transported (often on a daily and/or rotating basis) to meat processing companies and food packing firms in one of the main foci/semi-rural towns mentioned earlier.

Housing rental and transport costs were deducted from the employee's wages. This salary, in turn, was paid by the agency and not directly by the factory of employment. In a further twist, the agency was paid by the receptor company at the level of the minimum legal wage for the production work that was provided by the migrant. The agency then paid the migrant labourer a wage (minus the agent's deductions) at a basic level that it determined. Often, the money was paid 'cash in hand' and via a second intermediary who was invariably a native, Portuguese-speaking, charge-hand, who may also have extracted his/her 'cut' (or commission). (C) acknowledged this process whereby:

> the wages are identical for local and foreign employees [...] [and her] company pays the agencies [...] [that] then pay the foreign worker. Through the agencies though, the foreign workers only receive the basic rate.

As a result, the sum of money ultimately paid to the migrant worker could be significantly less than wages being paid to a local worker who was directly employed by the factory. However, as one moved along this schematic continuum, so the labour market changed from formalized to less formal, and then into an informal/'grey' area where regulatory controls were more difficult to enforce. Unsurprisingly, this sub-contracting arrangement became increasingly hierarchical and thus more complicated in its operation and led to allegations that migrant workers were being exploited. Indeed, many were now considered

---

[33] Kathryn Bell, Neil Jarman and Thomas Lefebvre, *Migrant Workers in Northern Ireland* (Belfast: Institute for Conflict Research, 2004), p. 54.

victims of a 'long hours/low pay' syndrome that has proliferated elsewhere in Britain.[34]

Problems in the Labour Market

The major feature to emerge from the investigation related to the employment situation, and more specifically, the issues of exploitation and harassment. These hazards were often perpetuated by intimidation and fear on the part of intermediaries. Indeed, in many respects these workers were dependent upon the 'generosity' of their labour agents but vulnerable to (unfair) dismissal and ejection from tied accommodation at short notice. (A), for example, alleged that:

> Portuguese people and other foreigners [...] were complaining that [Mr X, an employment agent] was bullying and threatening them [...]. I knew of them putting Portuguese out of their homes which they were renting off [Mr X], during the night, if they were going to shift jobs that were not a part of the [named] agency.

Rivalry, competitiveness and a desire to obtain (and retain) part of a lucrative share of employers' financial contributions were the main factors affecting the behaviour of these controlling agents. Indeed, it echoed a similar system operating in Portugal but relating to some Portuguese labour agents' nefarious treatment of Lusophone African immigrants during the 1990s.[35] There were further parallels with immigrants entering Portugal, given that they were carrying similar life experience backgrounds to those entering Northern Ireland. This was because the Portuguese emigrants possessed a strong work ethic and had family values at the root of their decision to emigrate.[36] In the latter case, these driving forces included a desire to earn money, remit savings, improve their lives and those of their family, educate their children, and broaden their horizons. Many of these migrants, therefore, made independent choices in order to maximize both their incomes and other opportunities within the constraints that they faced. This reflected a dual frame of reference that they carried with them.[37] In other words, they were engaged in a 'trade-off', whereby relatively 'poor' wages and difficult working conditions abroad were tolerated because the wage earned in Northern Ireland, for example, was higher than any potential earnings in their home country. Indeed, Portuguese workers appeared to accept their circumstances in deference to the remuneration that they received: sterling. This money could be converted into a relative fortune in euros when repatriated, thus helping to

---

[34] TUC, *Overworked, Underpaid and Over Here: Migrant Workers in Britain* (London: TUC, 2003).
[35] Martin Eaton, 'Portugal's Lusophone African Immigrants: Colonial Legacy in a Contemporary Labour Market', in *The Last Empire: Thirty Years of Portuguese Decolonisation*, ed. by Stewart Lloyd-Jones and António Costa Pinto (Bristol: Intellect, 2003), pp. 99–112 (p. 108).
[36] McGreevy and Bayne.
[37] Russell King, 'From Guestworkers to Immigrants: Labour Migration from the Mediterranean Periphery', in *The New Europe: Economy, Society and Environment*, ed. by David Pinder (Chichester: Wiley, 1998), pp. 263–80 (p. 270).

improve familial circumstances in their home areas. However, in extreme cases and according to (C), for example:

> If foreign workers have trained to a higher level and are working through an agency they still only receive the basic rate, so in some cases they were exploited through their agency.

This scenario was complicated and relative to the individual's circumstances since one person's 'self-exploitation' represented another person's 'trade-off'. (H), for instance, was previously a car mechanic in his native Brazil, where he

> made more money than most but this only allowed [him] to have a basic standard of living [at home]. It [was] nothing compared to what [he made] now [in Northern Ireland].

(H) explained that he currently had a specialist (food processing) job that meant receipt of 'a higher salary', and placed him in an even more advantageous position.

A related feature was the integration process that these migrant workers underwent in the face of wider societal issues such as racial tension, verbal abuse and sporadic violence.[38] The latter was, on occasions, a reciprocal process because there was some evidence of intimidation and violence being directed by Portuguese against fellow nationals. Indeed, some Portuguese 'work supervisors' were alleged to be coercing the contracted immigrant workforce into rejecting trade union membership and encouraging the Portuguese to inform on each other with respect to misdemeanours, both serious and trivial . The consequences were sometimes extreme, as (A) explained:

> I know a Portuguese guy who had a bottle smashed over his head. Also [name of agent] and his crowd treat Portuguese like slaves and carry out wrongful beatings, which I would class as racial.

Equally, there was some observational evidence of intimidation by Portuguese of the indigenous community (e.g. shoplifting, drugs supplying and casual violence). Conversely, there were instances of harassment of workers by locals, particularly in social interaction arenas such as public houses and nightclubs. Experiences amongst the respondents were mixed but the underlying theme was one of conflict. (H), for example, stated that:

> I had one or two problems with local people [...] mainly occurring on nights out in [a nearby] town.

(A) claimed that:

> one [Portuguese] guy was called a monkey because he was black and people call us smelly and think we are diseased. [Some] homes are targeted with petrol bombs.

---

[38] 'Portugueses Vítimas de Ataques Racistas na Irlanda do Norte', *Público*, 29 April 2002; Anon., 'Stabbing Appeal to Foreign Nationals', *Tyrone Today*, 3 February 2006, online at <http://findarticles.com/p/news-articles/tyrone-times-dungannon-northern-ireland/mi_7957/is_2006_Feb_3/stabbing-appeal-foreign-nationals/ai_n34571584/> [accessed 11 November 2009].

(D) spoke of 'some resentment towards the migrant workforce' and (E) detailed that:

> there were five [Portuguese] guys [...] [whose houses] are stoned and egged no matter where they move to within the town.

It appeared that the antagonism was not exclusively, therefore, the domain of the local resident/worker against the immigrant but more a two-way process reflecting confrontational attitudes on the part of some of the immigrant population (agents/supervisors/workers) against each other. A complex picture was clouded further by the alleged involvement of local paramilitary vigilantes looking to 'control' what they considered to be 'their' communities.[39] (E) stated:

> Most attacks [on property] are from [...] youth mobs that are linked to paramilitaries and it is the paramilitaries who control the attacks. Some of the houses, which are rented to Portuguese people, are paramilitary owned and these people [...] [then] demand £20 per week from the Portuguese who live in them to ensure their windows stay in [...] and that they receive no attacks.

This, of course, had a multiple impact since some Portuguese workers had monies deducted at source by the labour agent, and on occasions by their supervisor, paid rent to the (alleged paramilitary) 'landlord' and then had to pay protection money to the same 'landlord' to secure a safe living existence. When coupled with poor living conditions and multiple occupancy (E) attested that 'males and young workers tend to overcrowd terrace housing' (in Portadown), many Portuguese found themselves in difficult circumstances. Moreover, from a spatial perspective, many immigrants lived in rundown, dilapidated interface areas between unionist and nationalist communities. These workers were, therefore, often on the 'frontline' at times of heightened tension, such as during the Orange Order parading season each summer.

Community Responses

Another complication emerged, since the process of adaptation by Portuguese immigrants to the local society, and indeed, by local communities to the Portuguese (and other immigrant communities) has been slow. Mobilizations by organizations such as the NI district councils and agencies like the Citizens Advice Bureaux to help local integration efforts are only a recent development. In fairness, relative (statistical) invisibility within Northern Ireland meant it was difficult for the region's social services, for example, to help the workers. A simple lack of knowledge of an exact number of immigrants resulted in resourcing decisions often being ill-informed and poorly determined. It was also initially difficult to address issues such as efficient provision of English language classes, the proper distribution of interpreting and translating services,

---

[39] 'Petrol bomb attack was "racist"', *BBC News* (7 November 2004), online at <http://news.bbc.co.uk/1/hi/northern_ireland/3989801.stm> [accessed 11 November 2009].

or equitable access to health services, education facilities, jobs and social welfare benefit offices, and so on.

The situation, however, has changed with greater recognition and involvement through, for example, regional authorities and local councils providing interpreters and translations of documents. In this respect, a number of organizations have become proactive players.[40] The Department for Employment and Learning in NI, for example, has produced a Portuguese-language series of frequently asked questions on the role of employment agencies.[41] At the micro-scale, several simple but far-reaching transitory arrangements emerged in the local labour markets. (B) (referring to a national supermarket retailer) stated that:

> In the Dungannon store they put up signs in Portuguese for taxis and [one] manager was sent to learn Portuguese. In this [...] store we have an outside firm [which] acts as a translator and is [...] used when the customer requires one.

Other retailers specifically employed Portuguese personnel in their human resource department to assist with their recruitment process. This often facilitated direct employment strategies between a migrant worker and a specific company, thus removing the agent from the employment equation. (C) noted that:

> Within Personnel we have a Portuguese girl who assists in the [worker] interviews and also checks identity cards [for false representation and fraud].

In addition, the Police Service of Northern Ireland employed a civilian interpreter for the mid-Ulster area, and community-funded initiatives such as the South Tyrone Empowerment Programme (STEP) was utilized to support the immigrant community.[42] Migrant Workers Forums were set up in Craigavon and a community/voluntary partnership called ANIMATE (Action Now to Integrate Minority Access to Equality) was working on migrant worker issues in the Dungannon, Craigavon and Cookstown areas.[43] Campaigns aimed at disseminating an anti-racism message in the workplace were also instigated in Dungannon in the spring of 2006, using advertising on buses.[44] Moreover, a local newspaper, the *Tyrone Courier*, published a weekly column in Portuguese devoted to matters of local interest to the immigrants. This was tangible recognition of the contribution that the Portuguese workers have made; a point noted by (J)

---

[40] Agnieszka Martynowicz and Neil Jarman, *New Migration, Equality and Integration: Issues and Challenges for Northern Ireland* (Belfast: Equality Commission for NI, 2009).
[41] DELNI, *Regulamentações para Agências de Emprego e de Recursos Humanos* (Belfast: DELNI, 2008).
[42] Roisin Donaghy, 'Portuguese Praised for Contribution', *CommunityNI*, 20 June 2005, online at <http://www.communityni.org/news/portuguese-praised-contribution> [accessed 11 November 2009].
[43] Craigavon Borough Council, *CBC Community Relations Plan 2005–2006* (Craigavon: CBC, 2005).
[44] Dungannon and South Tyrone Borough Council, *Good Relations Audit and Strategic Plan 2006–2007* (Derry: Holywell Consultancy, 2006), p. 10.

when he stated that:

> there are more than two [nationalist and unionist] communities in Dungannon: the Portuguese are now a sizeable group and an important part of life in Dungannon.

In some respects the Portuguese emigrant experience in the province mimicked that found in rural parts of mainland Britain such as Lincolnshire, Norfolk and Suffolk. The situation they found themselves in was fluid and the immigrant group was rapidly expanding. Most new entrants were trying to shuffle up a conceptual 'socio-economic pyramid',[45] which was based upon relative levels of aspiration, wages and living conditions found in different parts of north-western Europe. When (A) was asked what factors made her decide to leave Portugal her answer was emphatic. In ontological terms she echoed the views of most workers: 'money'. In turn, even the minimum-working wage (minus agent's and other deductions)/basic wage earned locally was higher than could be made in Portugal. As (A) confirmed 'everything keeps going up in price, housing, clothes, food, etc. but the salary stays the same so it becomes unaffordable to live there'.

Northern Ireland was, ergo, an outwardly attractive location pulling workers into the province and providing jobs and financial rewards. On the downside, only the weather militated against even greater levels of satisfaction, since according to (A) 'it is very cold here'. Equally, the local education system (once the initial English language barrier had been overcome) offered first-generation migrant workers' children a much better prospect and quality of schooling than similar facilities found back home.[46] Indeed, the Portuguese in Northern Ireland quickly moved beyond a pioneer stage and were now settling with spouses/partners and/or children. As (E) attested 'there are 70 [Portuguese] kids now in school in Portadown: mostly in primary schools but there are a few attending secondary school'. All of these favourable conditions, therefore, had the potential to allow further improvement of the familial situation. Once again, they helped to justify the 'trade-off' associated with many of the immigrants' work experiences and living conditions, and their apparent willingness to tolerate the more negative aspects of their existence.

Conclusions

In summation, we have tentatively examined the scale, experiences and impacts of Portuguese migrant workers in Northern Ireland's agricultural/food processing labour market. Our analysis suggests that employment of Portuguese migrants, in Portadown, Dungannon, and other important market towns, has been significantly driven by employment agencies. This process has facilitated recruitment strategies, provided factories with a stable workforce, and

---

[45] Eaton, p. 109.
[46] David Newnham, 'Between Two Worlds', *Times Educational Supplement*, 28 February 2003.

counteracted many of the labour shortages associated with the rurally based food processing sectors. A new working pattern based upon segmentation of the labour market when supplemented by migrant workers has emerged. Equally, the role of agencies has brought adverse consequences for some migrants in terms of reduced pay and inferior working and living conditions compared to other (non-migrant) workers. However, it appeared that this often reflected a conscious decision-making process on the part of the migrant. Workers were willing to 'trade-off' personal inconveniences in deference to monetary remuneration, remittance value, and savings, all of which could be used to improve familial circumstances, both in Portugal, and increasingly, in Northern Ireland itself. As such, many Portuguese appeared to tolerate the dualistic operating and living conditions that they faced as well as the slowness associated with the pace of developmental change and the process of adaptation to, and on the part of, many local communities.

Consequently, the future for these types of immigrant is difficult to surmise. It may be that with growing numbers of migrant labourers and increasing evidence of family reconciliation then greater integration can be expected. Integration may take two forms. First, in terms of the community, and as we have observed, first-generation immigrant children are now settling in Northern Ireland's primary schools. With time it is expected that they will move into secondary school and the tertiary education sector. Moreover, it is likely that Portuguese community groups/associations will be established, and continue to grow. Hypothetically, they may come to mirror (on a smaller scale) the established Portuguese social communities found in London and parts of the Channel Islands, East Anglia and Manchester. Fledgling examples already exist in Dungannon where the weekend use of a local community centre together with a Portuguese-owned restaurant and a managed public house forms the hub for a local socialization/integration process to take place. Portadown has a public house with a strong Portuguese clientele, and a coffee house and shop selling Portuguese goods, which acts as an informal drop-in centre offering mutual advice, support and translation services. The town also has a Church specifically designed for Portuguese migrant workers and their families to attend (and according to E has a congregation of 'approximately fifty people attending at present'). More importantly, these initiatives are contributing to a relatively positive chain of feedback information that constitutes a key part of the strong worker migration trail that has now developed between Portugal and Northern Ireland.

Second, greater levels of integration can be anticipated in terms of the local labour market. Progress has been made, with some migrant workers now being directly employed by local companies rather than continuing to be linked to a labour agency. These workers are benefiting from minimum working wages, bonus payments, overtime, training opportunities, health and safety protection, English-language attainment, access to trade union membership, and closer immersion in the workforce and local economy. However, there is a danger that if labour agencies are not carefully regulated then the problems of exploitation, harassment and violence demonstrated in this article could continue to leave Portuguese immigrants exposed as a vulnerable group in a society not characterized by its tolerance of 'outsiders'.[47] The external spectre of violence is unlikely to go away completely and it is a disturbing prospect; one orchestrated by criminal paramilitary elements (both republican and loyalist) exerting what they see as 'control' over 'their' (both local, and increasingly immigrant) working-class communities.

Equally, as segmentation in the labour market continues and potential saturation point is neared with migrant workers continuing to locate in Northern Ireland and enter jobs that local workers are reluctant to take on, then it is possible that conflict will develop. There is already some observational evidence of friction developing between different groups of migrant workers (Portuguese and central and eastern Europeans, for example) competing for the same job vacancies in mid-Ulster. This antagonism may be exacerbated in the longer term in a four-way internecine 'Taking Our Jobs' tension between the local, Portuguese, central-, and east-European working groups. The issue is, once again, complicated because of debate over whether there is a finite limit to the number of jobs available in the agricultural/food-processing sector of Northern Ireland. It may be that saturation point is being reached or that economic slowdown and recession is having a greater than previously anticipated impact. On the other hand (and related to inferences from the survey on the part of interviewees B and E) respondents claimed that some local market towns (like Portadown) have been regenerated. They focused upon the positive contributions of migrant workers who have helped to improve local retail trade, boosted building, painting and decorating services, and produced re-investment, increases in jobs and sustained growth of factories.[48]

As a result, with time, co-operation and a level of tolerance, the Portuguese workers and their families could be a welcome addition to the establishment of multiculturalism and a multi-ethnic society within the region. Such a community already typifies large urban centres in the rest of Britain but the process is still in its infancy in Northern Ireland. Moreover, it is a largely unknown concept in many rural, market towns, and more economically peripheral parts of the province. The overcoming of this lack of experience of migrant labourers and their contributions will be a key factor in changing community relations and perceptions of the Portuguese. It is a feature that time will change but one that will require all parties to come together to discuss their similarities and differences. Given past experience, and an apparent hardening of attitudes

---

[47] Concordia, *Migrant Workers in Northern Ireland* (Dungannon: Concordia, 2006), p. 12.
[48] Department of Enterprise, Trade and Investment, 'Northern Ireland's Unemployment Rate Remains Low' (18 July 2007), online at <http://www.northernireland.gov.uk/news/news-deti/news-deti-july-2007/news-deti-180707-northern-irelands-unemployment.htm> [accessed 11 November 2009].

towards migrant workers,[49] there is no guarantee that this will happen. Because of this uncertainty, Portuguese migrant workers in Northern Ireland remain in a classical state of flux.

This article is a revised version of Martin Eaton, 'From Porto to Portadown: Portuguese Workers in Northern Ireland's Labour Market', *Portuguese Journal of Social Science*, 6, 3 (2007), 171–92. The author is grateful to Lara Blevins for her assistance with the fieldwork.

UNIVERSITY OF ULSTER

---

[49] DELNI, *Attitudes to Migrant Workers: Results from the Northern Ireland Omnibus Survey* (Belfast: DELNI, 2007), pp. 2–3.

Portuguese Migrant Workers in the UK: A Case Study of Thetford, Norfolk

JOSÉ CARLOS PINA ALMEIDA AND DAVID CORKILL

The Portuguese-speaking population resident in the UK has experienced considerable growth since the late 1990s. The high-water mark of this phase of Portuguese emigration came during the early years of the new century and lasted until the economic and financial crisis brought to an end over a decade of uninterrupted growth and prosperity. Although the Portuguese were amongst the vanguard of migrants entering the country in recent years, they have remained marginal to the research agenda, unlike their east- and central-European counterparts (collectively known as migrants from the A8/A2 countries) who arrived in substantial numbers after EU enlargement in 2004. This study attempts to rectify this by focusing on the Portuguese-speaking migrants, an ethnically diverse, multinational Lusophone grouping, many of whom were born outside Portugal. It explores questions related to migrant motivations, how migration and settlement occurred, integration and adaptation to the labour market and receptor society, as well as intra-community relations. In addition, it traces and analyses recent employment patterns and settlement trends among Portuguese migrant workers in eastern England. This particular region was chosen because it contains various points of migrant concentration, including Great Yarmouth, Swaffham, East Dereham, Boston and in particular Thetford in Norfolk, where Portuguese-speaking groups have become highly visible and well established.

Brettell points out that in Portugal a 'culture of migration' has developed in such a way that migration has become deeply ingrained in the repertoire of people's behaviours.[1] We conclude that when facing situations such as unemployment, the common response of many Portuguese is to emigrate, thereby underlining mobility as a core feature of the Portuguese migration phenomenon. The Portuguese have been settling and working in the UK since the 1950s but until recently their numbers were always small compared to those who opted to go to France, Switzerland, Luxembourg and elsewhere on the continent. As a consequence, when Portuguese migrants began entering the UK in increasing numbers, it represented a relatively new destination in the migratory trajectory and history of the Lusophone groups. Unlike the initial Portuguese incomers, who tended to settle in London and the south-east, a primary characteristic of this 'second immigration age' is their geographical spread across the country and

---

[1] Caroline Brettell, *Anthropology and Migration: Essays on Transnationalism, Ethnicity and Identity* (Walnut Creek, CA: Altamira, 2003).

the propensity for greater mobility and dispersion among the migrant population. Equally, their employment patterns are more diverse, with particular emphasis on agriculture and agriculture-related light industry. Importantly, these migrants spread into smaller towns and rural settlements that had little or no previous experience as receptors and consequently lacked established networks and integration infrastructures. Indeed, migrants have traditionally settled in urban areas,[2] this being the reason why, in the past, research into migration has focused on the larger cities and towns.

However, evidence from recent flows is that settlement patterns are far more dispersed both nationally and regionally, requiring a shift in and a reformulation of the research agenda. There is now a critical need to investigate the impact of migration and settlement of foreign-born workers in small town communities, often located within a rural or semi-rural environment. These locations are generally conservative, largely monocultural and often unaccustomed to dealing with cultural difference (apart, in the case of Thetford, from absorbing newcomers that in earlier decades formed part of the London overspill); this is because small towns in the UK are often characterized by their ageing populations, declining services and facilities, and out-migration, particularly of the younger members of the community. Apart from representing an opportunity for incoming migrants, these features also present challenges and issues that might be expected to vary from those experienced in the larger urban context.

Portuguese Migration into the UK

Portuguese emigration to the UK is relatively new. Although many Portuguese entered the UK during the 1950s and 1960s (the period known as the *guest worker era*), the scale of their migration there was considerably less than to other countries such as France and Germany. The UK only emerged as a significant destination during the resurgence in emigration flows dating from the late 1990s, when Portugal itself made the transition from being a source country of emigrants to being an immigrant receptor country. This resurgence in emigration seems to have coincided with a negative cycle in the Portuguese economy that started in 2001. According to data from the Portuguese National Statistical Office, the unemployment rate increased from 3.9 per cent in 2000 to 7.7 per cent in 2006.[3] Nevertheless, some parts of London such as the borough of Lambeth, and its ward of Stockwell in particular, have been home to Portuguese migrants for more than thirty years.[4] One recent estimate has put the number of Portuguese in this

---

[2] Michael Randall and John Salt, 'The Foreign-Born Population', in *Focus on People and Migration* (London: Office for National Statistics, 2005), pp. 131–51 (p. 135).

[3] José Carlos Pina Almeida, 'Citizens of the World: Migration and Citizenship of the Portuguese in the UK', *Portuguese Studies*, 23, 2 (2007), 208–29 (p. 213).

[4] Wenona Giles, 'Class, Gender and Race Struggles in a Portuguese Neighbourhood in London', *International Journal of Urban and Regional Research*, 15 (1991), 432–41 (p. 434). Maria João Nogueira and David Porteous, 'The socio-cultural characteristics and needs of a

part of London at 27,000,[5] but local community workers and migrant groups regard this figure as far too conservative. For example, João de Noronha, editor of the Portuguese-language newspaper circulated amongst Lusophone migrants in the UK, estimates that there are 350,000 Portuguese passport holders in Greater London alone.[6]

Estimating the overall size of the Portuguese population in the UK is also no easy task. Although there is a fairly wide range of data available from sources such as the National Statistical Office, consular registrations, the Labour Force Survey and National Insurance records, figures and statistics tend to be extremely variable: estimates of the total number of Portuguese living in the UK range from 80,000 to 700,000 depending on the source consulted. Noronha, whose figures are premised on the number of Council Tax payers, using a multiplier of four persons per household, claims a somewhat inflated figure of 716,400 in the UK during 2009. However, despite the disparities, what these different sources do agree on is the substantial increase in the number of arrivals since 2000.[7]

With regard to employment, the Labour Force Survey suggests that together with their southern-European counterparts from Spain, Italy and Greece, workers from Portugal are engaged predominantly in manual employment. Data from National Insurance Number registrations also revealed a fairly young population: 46 per cent of the total registrations recorded in the period 2001–05 were made by applicants between twenty and twenty-nine years of age. In the Labour Force Survey carried out between 2000 and 2004, the Portuguese respondents who had arrived after 1990 were also generally young, thus mirroring the usual trend of new migrant groups, in which around 90 per cent of the population are below forty-five years of age.[8]

A Lusophone Multinational Group

A signature characteristic of Portuguese-speaking groups in the UK is their diversity in terms of origin. Previous research has found that around 30 per cent of Portuguese nationals registered with the Portuguese consular services in London were people born outside Portugal.[9] The following six countries appear to be highly significant as birthplaces of Portuguese nationals thus registered:

Portuguese community in south London', in *The Education of Portuguese Children in Britain: Insights from Research and Practice in England and Overseas*, ed. by Guida Abreu, Tony Cline and Hannah Lambert (London: Department of Basic Education and Calouste Gulbenkian Foundation, 2003), pp. 51–74 (p. 53).

[5] 'Every race, colour, nation and religion on earth — part three', *The Guardian*, 21 January 2005. Available online at <http://www.guardian.co.uk/uk/2005/jan/21/race.britishidentity> [accessed 11 November 2009].

[6] *As Notícias*, 60, 29 May 2009.

[7] Almeida, p. 227.

[8] Sarah Kyambi, *Beyond Black and White: Mapping New Immigrant Communities* (London: IPPR, 2005), p. 56.

[9] Almeida, p. 217.

Angola, India, Mozambique, Brazil, South Africa and China (Macau). This finding reflects the fact that Portugal maintained its empire until as late as the mid-1970s and these migrants often lived in Portugal for some time before moving to the UK. Subsequently, Portugal's accession to the European Union in 1986 permitted those colonial subjects who possessed a Portuguese passport to gain entry to other member states.

While the current emigration wave comprises significantly larger numbers of migrants entering the UK, it also shares certain common elements with the previous emigration phase, discussed earlier. Then and now, the principal motivation for migration continues to be the high rate of unemployment back in Portugal. Thus, the inability to find work in Portugal during a period of economic recession has acted as a catalyst in the decision to emigrate. During the 1990s there were large-scale closures of Portuguese factories resulting from global competition and rising domestic costs, including higher wages. The absence of alternative employment meant that redundant workers and new labour market entrants faced a bleak future. The majority of those workers who decided to migrate were male; women constituted only about a quarter of the total, indicating a gender selective migration in reaction to the crisis in Portugal,[10] and replicating the patterns from the 1960s and 1970s. In addition to being predominantly male, the migrant population continues to comprise mainly young people of working age. The majority is relatively poorly educated and low skilled, in contrast to many of the east-European migrants that followed them into the UK. And like the earlier generations who came to the UK, most do not have a good working command of the English language. Work schedules and the prevalence of overtime often preclude attendance at language classes, or other attempts to rectify this deficiency. In terms of recent patterns and trends of migration flows in Europe, there are thus some remarkable parallels with the earlier 'guest worker' phase after the Second World War.[11]

East Anglia: A New Destination

East Anglia is an important agricultural region that became a magnet for the Portuguese and other migrant workers because of the excellent employment opportunities in the bacon, chicken and turkey packing industries, in flower picking and in the harvesting of fruit and vegetables. The Portuguese were amongst the earliest arrivals, but were quickly followed by considerable numbers of eastern Europeans, from Poland, Lithuania, Estonia, Latvia and Russia. There was a high demand for labour because local firms were experiencing considerable difficulties in recruiting for seasonal work that often required large numbers of workers for short periods of time or, in the case of turkey farms and factories,

[10] Jorge Malheiros, *SOPEMI Report: Portugal* (Paris: OECD, 2005).
[11] John Salt and José Carlos Almeida, 'International Migration in Europe: Patterns and Trends since the mid-1990s', *Revue Européenne des Migrations Internationales*, 22 (2006), 155–75 (p. 173).

only in the pre-Christmas period. The local workforce was not able to cope with the demands made by these labour-intensive industries. The majority of the local population was extremely reluctant to accept the low-paid temporary work on offer, and even when local people were prepared to take this work on, their sparse scattering across the region meant that the inadequate local public transportation system struggled to serve them all. Given such deficiencies, employers began to seek to engage migrant workers, either through employment agencies or via in-house recruitment.

In Norfolk, dense concentrations of Portuguese workers quickly sprung up in Thetford, Great Yarmouth, Swaffham and East Dereham. This study focuses on Thetford, a small market town in the west Norfolk district of Breckland. In the 1960s the town was designated for London overspill and by the 1990s the population had reached 20,000. However, by 2006 the influx of foreign-born migrants had boosted the population to more than 28,000, posing new challenges and problems for the rural community.[12] The Portuguese migrants who established themselves in Thetford soon grew to comprise just under one third of the total population.

Migrations are managed and influenced today by different interests, agencies and institutions, including the politics of nationhood and citizenship. The nationality law has now been revised (2006), but data available shows that a significant number of Portuguese nationals living in the UK were born outside Portugal, having acquired Portuguese nationality either as residents of other parts of the Portuguese empire, before its dissolution in 1974 (Macau was handed over to China in 1999), or by claiming Portuguese descent. As a colonial power, Portugal created an inclusive model of citizenship as a means to integrate their colonial subjects, but after the dissolution of the empire the Law of Nationality (1981) shifted from being based primarily on *jus soli*, granting citizenship to those born in Portuguese territory, including parts of Africa, to *jus sanguinis*, which granted citizenship to people of Portuguese descent. In the context of the Schengen agreement and free movement in the European Union, possession of a member-state nationality became a very important asset for those who wanted to come to live and work in Europe. Indeed, the Brazilian ambassador made public reference to the fact that many Brazilians had taken out Portuguese citizenship in order to enter Europe. (Likewise many were able to apply for Italian nationality because of the large numbers of Italians who had migrated from Italy to Brazil in the nineteenth and early twentieth centuries.) The rules on nationhood and citizenship have therefore clear political implications for governments, groups and individuals, raising questions concerning existing notions of belonging and current understandings of citizenship and national affiliations.

Following a quantitative analysis of the available data on Portuguese migration to the UK, fieldwork was carried out in London and in Thetford. This included

---

[12] Claudia Schneider and Deborah Holman, *A Profile of Migrant Workers in the Breckland Area* (Thetford: Keystone Development Trust, 2005), pp. 1–15.

interviews with migrants in order to understand the varied trajectories, motivations and strategies. Gatekeepers such as community workers, non-governmental migrant organizations and local authorities and Portuguese representatives in the UK were also interviewed. In addition, focus group discussions were organized to explore issues raised in individual interviews and to gather further data on the collective representations of identity. All interviews were carried out by the authors, mostly in Portuguese. The names used are fictitious throughout.

Fieldwork carried out amongst migrant workers in East Anglia revealed that a proportion of the Portuguese nationals residing in that area were born in Brazil but had acquired Portuguese nationality. A case in point is Gabriela, who came to the UK in 2006. She arrived with her parents after their business in Brazil was forced to close. They travelled to Portugal with the help of family members and then relocated to England on the advice of friends. In this process, possession of Portuguese nationality proved vital for the family:

> O meu avô era português e ele foi para o Brasil com nove anos de idade. Nós todos conseguimos a nacionalidade através dele [...]. Quando se trata de assinar o contrato eu sou portuguesa. Mas na fábrica todo mundo me conhece como a brasileira.[13]

> [My grandfather was Portuguese and he went to Brazil when he was nine years old. Through him we all got nationality [...]. When it comes to signing my contract, I am Portuguese. But in the factory I am known as the Brazilian girl.]

This instrumental use of Portuguese nationality was one of the more interesting issues to emerge from many of the interviews with migrants. Indeed, it often provoked a degree of resentment among those who believe that Portuguese citizenship should be reserved for the 'real' Portuguese:

> Há muitos brasileiros e outros por aqui com papéis portugueses mas esses não são realmente portugueses.[14]

> [There are a lot of Brazilians and other people around here with Portuguese papers but they are not really Portuguese.]

> Se eles nasceram em Cabo Verde, eles não são portugueses. Como um angolano que nasceu em Angola é angolano. Agora há aqueles que nasceram em Portugal mas que mantiveram a raça [...] a maioria via Lisboa [...]. Um angolano tem que chegar aqui com um passaporte, um visto, um trabalho. Então, alguns vão para Portugal, conseguem arranjar documentos falsos, e vêm para aqui e começam a trabalhar. Um angolano é como um brasileiro. Ele não pertence à Comunidade Europeia portanto tem de chegar aqui com um certo estatuto. Se não vem com um certo estatuto, eles arranjam documentos falsos. Outros viveram em Portugal alguns anos e fizeram o mesmo que eu fiz: precisavam de mudar as suas vidas.[15]

---

[13] Gabriela, 21 years old, resident in the UK for one year.
[14] Joaquim, 55 years old, resident in the UK for four years.
[15] David, resident in the UK for eight years.

[If they were born in Cape Verde, they are not Portuguese. Like an Angolan who was born in Angola is Angolan. Now there are those who were born in Portugal but have kept up their [African] ethnicity [...] the majority come via Lisbon [...]. An Angolan has to arrive here with a passport, with a visa, with a job. So, some go to Portugal, they manage to get false documents, and then they come here to start working. An Angolan is like a Brazilian. He does not belong to the European Community and so he has to come with a particular status. If he does not come under a certain status, they get false documents. Others have lived in Portugal some years and have done the same as I did: they needed to change their lives.]

The persistence of this contradiction highlights the tension between the Luso-tropical discourse and reality, even in a diaspora context:

Vemos claramente que há uma cortina, uma distância entre africanos e continentais.[16]

[We see clearly that there is a curtain, a distance, between Africans and Portuguese.]

However, other interviewees maintained the familiar discourse that the Portuguese always mix easily with other peoples:

Os portugueses são mais maleáveis, mais adaptáveis [...] o português sempre encaixa onde quer que vá. Mas outros não [...] Se houve um bom colonizador, foi Portugal.[17]

[The Portuguese are more malleable, more adaptable [...] the Portuguese always fits in wherever he goes. But not others! [...] If there was a good colonizing country, it was Portugal.]

This is an example of the dominant self-perception amongst the Portuguese, reconstructing the idea of ethnic and racial harmony in a Lusophone transnational space where many peoples share a common language and culture, in this case in a diaspora context.

In the UK, however, the local authorities and the receptor population are unable to differentiate between these different groups and the label '3P migrants' (referring to their predominant activities: picking, plucking and packing) is usually applied to the whole Lusophone group. However, their impact on a particular settlement area should not be underestimated. An INTRAN report referred to Portuguese as the second most spoken language after English in Norfolk.[18] According to local council sources, around 8000 Portuguese-speakers were living in Thetford in 2007, mostly employed in agriculture and the food processing industries. Local community workers report that although many came with the intention of staying for a short period, the rate of settlement was relatively high, as the following comment by a community worker demonstrates:

---

[16] Manuel, 52 years old, resident in the UK for four years.
[17] Luís, 67 years old, resident in England for three years.
[18] Lynn Jervis-Chafaa, *Voluntary Sector INTRAN Pilot: Project Evaluation and Recommendations* (Norwich: Norwich and Norfolk Voluntary Services, 2006), p. 4.

A comunidade está muito bem estabelecida. Temos negócios, restaurantes, cafés, as pessoas estão a comprar casas. Portanto, se bem que muitas pessoas vêm com a intenção de ficar um ou dois anos, há muitos que estão a assentar, os seus filhos vão à escola, e eles acabam por ficar. E muitos vêm para se reunir com a sua família e trazem os seus amigos.[19]

[The community is very well established. We have businesses, restaurants, cafés, people are buying houses. So, although many people come with the intention of staying one or two years, many are settling down, their children go to school, and they end up staying. And many people now come to be reunited with their family and bring their friends.]

Given the high numbers, the Keystone Development Trust founded META (Multilingual and European Thetford Association, later renamed Mobile Europeans Taking Action) to work as an agency for the integration of both Portuguese and eastern-European migrants, by providing support to migrants seeking the necessary documentation, work permits, housing etc. This initiative attracted government funding in 2005 and has since been joined by the European Challenge, an organization originating within the group that offers translation, legal and other services.

Migration and the Labour Market

Initially, many migrants were recruited directly, in Portugal. Advertisements in Portuguese newspapers attracted unskilled male workers to the food processing factories and to the agricultural industries. Normally, these advertisements promised prospective workers a good salary, transport and accommodation, thus building up expectations that often were not met:

Normalmente eram os homens que vinham. E eles deixavam as famílias. A intenção era poupar algum dinheiro para levar para Portugal ou mandar para casa. Isto há cinco ou seis anos atrás [...]. Há uma agência na zona que por alguma razão já mudou de nome algumas vezes. Eles deixam gente numa situação realmente desesperada. Um homem suicidou-se no ano passado porque é uma agência que contrata gente que não fala inglês e portanto têm controlo sobre eles, depois dão-lhe uma casa e transporte [...]. Mas o controlo que têm permite situações como a deste senhor que era pago apenas o suficiente para pagar a renda. Ele não tinha sequer dinheiro para comprar comida. Estava só, não tinha família aqui e meteu-se numa situação tão desesperada que decidiu suicidar-se.[20]

[Normally it was the men who came. They would leave their families. The intention was to save a bit of money to take to Portugal or to send home. This was some five or six years ago [...]. There is an agency in the area that for some reason has changed its name a few times. They leave people in a really desperate situation. A man committed suicide last year, because it is an

---

[19] Maria, local community worker.
[20] Maria, local community worker.

agency that hires people who do not speak English so they have control over them, then they give them a house and transport [...]. But their control allows situations like this man who was being paid only enough to cover the rent. He did not even have any money to buy food. He was alone, did not have any family here and he got into such a desperate situation that he decided to commit suicide.]

The degree of control exerted by employers even extends to the retention of identification papers such as passports and other documents. The Gangmasters Licensing Act introduced in 2004 by the British government represented an attempt to prevent such abuses, but stories of exploitation by intermediaries, often Portuguese recruiters, continued to emerge. High expectations soon crumbled as the migrant realized that the promises made in the job interview had failed to materialize once in the UK:

> Eu passei por tudo o que as pessoas normalmente passam quando vêm para aqui. Respondi a um anúncio num jornal e fui entrevistado no [centro comercial] Colombo e depois de duas semanas eu vim para aqui [...]. Nunca houve nenhum contrato, eles eram portugueses mas trabalhavam para uma agência do norte do País de Gales. Éramos onze ou doze e quando vimos as condições [...] não tinham nada que ver com o que nos tinham dito. Eles disseram que o alojamento etc. seria pago, mas depois dás contigo num quarto com outra pessoa, numa casa sem água — é complicado [...] e eles não explicam nada disto às pessoas que vêm para aqui. É chocante. O que lês é uma coisa e o que vês quando chegas aqui é completamente diferente [...]. Eu falo bem o inglês mas muita gente não sabe falar e é uma grande barreira, as pessoas não sabem onde se dirigir ou o que fazer [...].[21]

> [I went through everything what people normally go through when they come here. I answered an advert in a newspaper and was interviewed in Colombo [a Lisbon shopping mall] and after two weeks I came here [...]. There was never any contract, they were Portuguese but worked for an agency in north Wales. There were eleven or twelve of us and when we saw the conditions [...] they were completely at odds with what they had told us. They said that accommodation etc. would be paid, but then you find yourself in a room with another person, in a house without water — it is tricky [...] and they don't explain any of this to the people who come here. It is shocking. What you read is one thing, and what you see once you get here is completely different [...]. I speak good English but many people can't speak it and it's a huge barrier, people don't know where to go or what to do [...].]

The above respondent, Hélder, works as a recruiter. He confirms that most Portuguese take relatively low paid jobs in the UK, but that the pay is still better than in Portugal. In Thetford, an unskilled job in a meat factory might pay around £800–£1000 per month. This compares favourably with a comparable salary in Portugal of around 400 euros per month, the minimum wage in Portugal, and equivalent to approximately £350.

---

[21] Hélder, entrepreneur, 24 years old, resident in Thetford for four years.

Some companies such as Bernard Matthews (BM) have their own recruitment offices in Portugal. Locals are invited to apply for interview through advertisements in Portuguese newspapers. Group interviews take place and all participants are hired initially for one month. An assessment is made after the first month and, depending on the results of the evaluation, an extended contract of six months may be offered. Fifty-one-year-old Rui attended one of these interviews. He considered moving to the UK or to Holland but changed his mind for family reasons and remained in Portugal, working with BM Foods to recruit Portuguese workers for the UK and Holland. He revealed that, in the case of Bernard Matthews:

> No mês de experiência, o salário seriam cerca de 250 euros por semana, depois das despesas. Isto por 39 horas de trabalho. Depois, se quiseres fazer mais horas, essas seriam pagas a 6,75 euros. Os sábados seriam pagos a 150 por cento e os domingos a 200 por cento. Não é mau. Se consegues fazer horas extra [...].

> [In the trial month, the salary would be around 250 euros per week, after expenses. This is for 39 hours work. Then, if you want to do more hours, those would be paid at 6.75 euros. Saturdays would be paid at 150 per cent and Sundays at 200 per cent. It's not bad. If you manage to do extra hours [...].]

However, other migrants come to the UK without a work contract or any dealings with a recruitment agency, as Rui, speaking from Portugal, attests:

> RUI: Muita gente vai para Inglaterra sem qualquer contrato e trabalham principalmente em restaurantes. Se as pessoas sabem falar inglês, podem ser empregados de mesa; se não sabem, ajudam na cozinha [...]. Há uma pessoa aqui (que não vou dizer o nome porque o que faz pode ser ilegal) que já recrutou centenas de pessoas. Um dos seus patrões também é daqui e ele recruta para uma cadeia de hotéis que também tem hotéis em Espanha [...].
> ENTREVISTADOR: Então, está muita gente a sair do país?
> RUI: Ai, sim, sim [...]. Está a ver, há muito desemprego por aqui. Se és jovem, eu não aconselho às pessoas a ficar em Portugal. Só agora há pouco tempo comecei a falar desta companhia dos perus e já tenho gente de cinquenta e mais anos que querem ir porque aqui não têm qualquer hipótese de conseguir trabalho [...]. São pessoas que estão a frequentar cursos de formação profissional [para desempregados] e ganham 200 euros [por mês]. Como é que eles podem cuidar de uma família com 200 euros?[22]

> [RUI: A lot of people go to England without any contract and work mainly in restaurants. If people can speak English, they can be waiters; if they don't, they help in the kitchen. [...]. There is a person from here (I am not going to say the name because what he does might be illegal) who has already placed hundreds of people. One of his bosses is from here too and he recruits for a hotel chain that also has hotels in Spain [...].
> INTERVIEWER: So, a lot of people are leaving the country?

---

[22] Rui, 51 years old.

RUI: Oh, yes, yes [...]. You know, there's a lot of unemployment around here. If you're young, I don't advise people to stay in Portugal. Just a short time ago I started to speak about this turkey company and already I've got people in their 50s and older that want to go because here in Portugal they don't have any chance of getting work. [...]. These people are on training courses [for the unemployed] earning 200 euros [per month]. How can they take care of the family on 200 euros?]

The arrival of many migrants from Poland and other eastern-European countries appears to be severely limiting employment opportunities for the Portuguese.[23] Along with this increased competition from eastern-European migrants, employment opportunities have become more limited as factories in East Anglia face mounting economic difficulties. Factory closures occurred during 2007 in Brandon and in Bury St Edmunds where more than a thousand Portuguese workers were employed. The outbreak of avian flu in a Bernard Matthews factory in Lowestoft, in the same year, threatened the jobs of hundreds of Portuguese workers, while Tulip Food Service Ltd in Thetford eventually closed down in 2009 with the loss of 300 Portuguese jobs. The declining demand for labour was confirmed by Hélder, the entrepreneur who has been resident in Thetford for four years: 'I had about 100 people working for me. Now I have around 20.'

The myth of return is deeply embedded in the Portuguese psyche. However, for many migrants facing redundancy or fewer job opportunities the prospect of return is unappealing. According to local community workers, many refuse to go back even when unemployed because of

orgulho, e também porque eles dizem que em Portugal a situação está igual, então porquê regressar? Não merece a pena e não resolveria nada.[24]

[pride, and also because they say that in Portugal the situation is the same, so why go back? It's not worth the trouble and it wouldn't solve anything.]

According to local recruiters and community workers, the migrant profile has recently undergone a slight modification even though employment opportunities have been contracting. Since 2004, a number of older migrants have started to arrive. In many cases, they are the parents of couples who were already settled here and they come over to carry out childcare duties, looking after their grandchildren whilst the parents work full-time. There has also been an increase in highly qualified migrants, such as doctors, teachers and lawyers who have had to settle for unskilled jobs in the food processing and packaging industries rather than carry out their professional duties. Nevertheless, it remains the case that migrants are generally young and unskilled workers, holding low-paid jobs.

---

[23] Ranald Richardson, Cheryl Conway and Stuart Dawley, *Assessing the Local and Regional Impacts of International Migration* (Newcastle: Centre for Urban and Regional Development Studies, Newcastle University, 2006). Accessed online at <http://www.ncl.ac.uk/curds/publications/pdf/A8Final.pdf>.
[24] Maria, local community organizer.

Transnational Mobility

Manuela Marques and Margarida Aguiar both comment that the Portuguese often see themselves as a people comprising different groups, geographically dispersed and forming a cosmopolitan diaspora, while retaining an umbilical cord linking them to the European motherland.[25] Our fieldwork in East Anglia confirms that the Portuguese group still maintains very close links with Portugal. Local cultural associations such as META organize celebrations of the main festival dates, such as Portuguese national day; the latest celebrations included not only the traditional folk dance from a local *rancho folclórico*, but also African dances from local youngsters. People keep close links with relatives and family in Portugal, not least through internet contact, and many take advantage of readily available and affordable air travel to visit Portugal several times a year. This might appear to contradict some of the attitudes about return referred to earlier, but it reflects the strategies and processes by which migrants adjust to the realities of migration.

It is also evident that the Portuguese diaspora is highly mobile and many migrant workers are prepared to move from one country to another in search of better job prospects. For example, Miguel, who is 34 years old, came from Holland where he had been working in the flower industry. His family joined him shortly after he first arrived. David spent two years working in Germany and returned to Portugal, where he lived for seven years before entering the UK. Manuel, who is now 52 years old, went to Venezuela when he was 17 years old. After 21 years, he returned to Portugal to escape the political instability, business uncertainty and personal security concerns. Unfortunately, his experience of life in Portugal was an unhappy one, and a family member who had moved directly from Venezuela to the UK persuaded Miguel to join him. However, he still harbours fond memories of the time spent in Venezuela:

> Os emigrantes vivem como ciganos. Hoje estamos aqui, amanhã já estamos noutro sítio. Mudamos de um país para outro por causa dos filhos, já que nós já estamos a ficar velhos. Eu não me surpreenderia se num ou dois anos eu já não esteja aqui, porque eu gostaria de morrer na Venezuela.[26]

> [Emigrants live like gypsies. We are here today, gone tomorrow. We move from one country to another country because of our children, since we're already getting old. I wouldn't be surprised if in one or two years' time I might not be here, because I would like to die in Venezuela.]

As we have commented above, the competition for jobs has recently increased with the arrival of many well-qualified migrants from eastern Europe. One of the

---

[25] Manuela Aguiar, *O País das Migrações sem Fim* (Lisbon: Cartográfica, 1999). Margarida Marques, 'Singularidade nacional e construção da cidadania: algumas reflexões sobre a difícil incorporação dos imigrantes na sociedade portuguesa', working paper (Lisbon: SociNova/Migrações: 2004), p. 1.

[26] Manuel, 52 years old, resident in the UK for four years.

responses from the Portuguese is to migrate yet again:

> Os que estão aqui e não conseguiram atingir os seus objectivos estão a ir para Espanha. Só no mês passado, houve muita gente a ir embora. Eu conheço pelo menos dez pessoas que foram [...], os empregos lá são muito bons. A maioria encontra trabalho nos hotéis onde podem ganhar 1200 euros. Aqui eles tiram £800 mas os custos de vida são muito mais altos se compararmos com Espanha. Lá conseguem uma casa por 400 euros, algumas até com piscina e tudo [...], portanto lá têm uma vida melhor. E também há o clima.[27]

> [The ones who are here and didn't manage to achieve their goals are going to Spain. Last month alone there were loads of people leaving. I know at least ten people who have gone [...], the jobs there are very good. The majority find work in hotels where they can earn 1200 euros. Here they get around £800 but living expenses are much higher compared to Spain. There they can get a house for 400 euros, some even with a swimming pool and all that [...], so they have a better life there. And there's the climate too.]

This secondary movement to Spain does not appear to be mediated by the same kind of factors that caused the concentration of Portuguese in Thetford. Existing social networks within the Portuguese group provide help and support, mainly through family and friends at various stages in the migration, settlement and job-seeking processes; furthermore, close transnational relationships exist amongst the groups. For example, Antónia, who is 39 years old, was born in Cape Verde and went to Portugal with her parents when she was nine. She has family in Luxembourg, Italy and France. She worked in Italy for a while but has lived in the UK for the last five years.

An indicator of the importance of networks in different countries is the sight of large number of foreign cars during holiday times in the areas of Lisbon where the migrant population is concentrated. These are cars owned by Cape Verdeans working in Holland or in Italy, or emigrants from Guinea-Bissau working in France who are visiting their families in Portugal. This and many other cases suggest that community networks are active even transnationally, despite the different individual strategies and patterns.

Conclusions

Much research remains to be done on the issues surrounding Portuguese migration to the UK, not least on the impact of the current economic recession and on its influence on decisions regarding integration or return. Reports in the media appear to indicate that eastern-European migrants have begun to return home in growing numbers as layoffs and fewer job opportunities combine with a devalued currency to make the UK a less obviously attractive destination.[28]

---

[27] Hélder.
[28] Under the headline 'More East Europeans leaving UK' the BBC reported a doubling of the numbers returning home (BBC News, 20 May 2009). Available online at <http://news.bbc.co.uk/1/hi/uk/8059122.stm>

In part this is a media concoction, and headlines such as '1000 Poles quit every week' (*The Scotsman*) and 'Eastern bloc exodus' (*Daily Mail*) ignored the fact that new arrivals had, in fact, ensured that there was a net increase.[29] An interesting comparison would be to evaluate whether the Portuguese have responded in a similar fashion. Given that Portuguese migrants tend to be extremely mobile it would be surprising if there were no reduction in the size of the Portuguese-speaking group as a result of the economic downturn. However, a number of factors may militate against a mass exodus. One is the continuing problems faced by the Portuguese economy itself, since it has been pushed even deeper into recession by the global downturn. Another is the fact that the agricultural sector in the UK has not been affected by the credit crunch in the same way as motor manufacturers and other high-value producers. Indeed, the UK consumer has continued to spend on food items and, to some extent, both agricultural producers and retailers have been protected from the worst of the recession. A third factor is that roots have been put down. Although the conventional wisdom is that the 2008 crisis halted the wave of immigration to the UK, evidence is emerging that the downturn in numbers which followed the big rise in the early part of the decade may have been only temporary. National Insurance Number registrations in 2008/09 indicate that the numbers have begun to rise again quite sharply. The infrastructure of a diaspora that embraces ethnic businesses, cultural associations and both local authority and voluntary agencies may well ensure that, despite difficult economic circumstances, a substantial Lusophone presence continues to be a feature of life in Norfolk and the east of England.

A modified version of this paper will appear in 2010 in *Immigrants & Minorities*.

MANCHESTER METROPOLITAN UNIVERSITY

---

[29] 21 May 2009.

Migrant Identities, Sociolinguistic and Sociocultural Practices: Portuguese and Spanish Migrations to the South Coast of England

Jaine Beswick and Alicia Pozo-Gutiérrez

Introduction

This paper presents research based around Bournemouth, in Dorset, aimed at mapping out and characterizing the presence of Portuguese and Spanish groups and communities in this south-coast English town. By adopting an interdisciplinary perspective, we focus on both the context that marked the arrival of Portuguese and Spanish migrants in this area and on overt manifestations of their identification patterns that are visible and perceivable in the public sphere, such as linguistic, social and cultural practices. This enables us to explore the relationship between language use and evolving identification attitudes and strategies adopted along different stages of the migratory process.

Contextualizing Portuguese and Spanish Migrations to the UK

For the purposes of this study, the distinction between Spanish and Portuguese migrants (both from Madeira and mainland Portugal) was determined by the identification and visibility of their geographical configuration. Whilst the Spanish presence was hardly perceptible and greatly dispersed across Bournemouth and surrounding areas of Dorset and Hampshire, the Portuguese presence was easily identifiable and highly concentrated around specific areas of Bournemouth, which became the primary area of the study, given the willingness of informants to take part in the research. We also identified a significant Brazilian presence in specific physical urban spaces of the town and in the articulation of certain sociocultural and sociolinguistic practices which often overlapped with the Portuguese presence. However, this will not be discussed here, as it forms the context of a later paper.

Before we outline the conceptual frames that guide our analysis and the discussion of our findings, we will present a brief historical outline of the initial settlement of the migrant groups under consideration. As part of a wider European migratory flow, the socio-economic dynamics that marked the European post-war period entailed, on the one hand, a high demand for the foreign labour needed to fuel the recuperation of north-western European economies (that of the UK amongst them), and on the other, a surfeit of labour emanating from southern European and Mediterranean countries, such as Portugal and Spain. Portuguese and Spanish migrations to and settlement in the UK also span a period of significant social and political flux, marked, amongst other factors, by the gradual re-incorporation of these countries into the international community after decades of isolationist policies engendered by dictatorial regimes in place up until the mid 1970s, and by subsequent processes of Europeanization and democratic transition in both countries.

This paper focuses on Portuguese and Spanish migrants who experienced what we understand as long-term or mid-term settlements. These migratory trajectories began whilst Portugal and Spain were under military dictatorship and continued from the early years of democracy through to the period soon after these countries joined the EEC. At each of these phases, we will demonstrate that the sociopolitical contexts of the migrations are comparable.

Theoretical Approach

Our theoretical approach draws from various models that frame migrants' incorporation into their receptor societies, and focuses on the impact that migration has had on the sense of identification and belonging. We explore the tension between strategies that migrants adopt in order to become inserted and functional in their receptor society, and the strategies that they adopt in order to preserve certain ethnic sociolinguistic and sociocultural traits throughout different phases of their migration cycle. In particular, we focus on the role of the autochthonous language, either to emphasize or to underplay a group's linguistic and social differentiation.

The classic model of assimilation,[1] dominant in migration discourses and policies until the mid 1960s, when the Spanish subjects of this study were beginning to arrive and settle in the UK, proposed that migrants committed themselves to being acculturated, absorbed and assimilated into the receptor societies by consciously breaking their ties and severing all links with their countries of origin. According to this model, achieving cultural homogeneity was considered necessary in order to maintain national stability, even if this resulted in the loss of migrants' sociocultural and sociolinguistic values.

The multicultural or anti-assimilationist model[2] offered an alternative paradigm based on the differentialist discourse that was to pervade immigration issues, practices and debates in the 1980s and 1990s, the time when the majority of the Portuguese migrants under consideration in this paper arrived and settled in Bournemouth. The main argument was centred upon the need to maintain social, cultural and linguistic diversity, arguing that its loss may have a negative effect on the minority community and the perception of its autochthonous ethnicity.

[1] For an early conceptualization of the assimilationist model, see Milton Myron Gordon, *Assimilation in American Life* (Oxford: Oxford University Press, 1964).
[2] For a conceptualization of the multicultural model, see John Rex, *Race and Ethnicity* (Milton Keynes: Open University Press, 1986).

Within the last two decades, the concept of transnationalism has become increasingly relevant to migration studies in general, and it has particularly relevance to this study if we are to offer a comparative evaluation of the sociolinguistic and sociocultural practices of both Spanish and Portuguese migrants today. It is now widely accepted that contemporary migration and settlement patterns are no longer necessarily determined by a definitive break from the home country, nor are they necessarily determined by the maintenance of discrete ethnic groupings within the receptor society. The transnational framework which emerged in the early 1990s was a useful concept for describing the exchanges that ensue from prolonged movement across frontiers between countries, and thus proposed that relationships and ties may be established and sustained between migrants and both their places of origin and the receptor society, both of which are subject to continual appraisal and evaluation.[3]

Recent reformulations of the assimilationist model and the critiques of the transnationalist model propose that migrants have a more proactive role in these processes than previously thought.[4] Kivisto for example, argues that transnationalism is simply a variant, not an alternative to traditional assimilation concepts. Notwithstanding the complex power relations ingrained in society and the limitations that these impose, Kivisto argues that at the same time as transmigrants are working at maintaining links and connections with their home countries, they are also actively and selectively engaged in the process of acculturation to the receptor society, along the lines proposed by Portes, Guaranizo and Landolt's notion of segmented assimilation and sociocultural transnationalism.[5] In other words, migrants may be simultaneously engaged in the multidimensional process of preserving certain ethnic, sociocultural and sociolinguistic practices, whilst divesting themselves of others, and at the same time adopting alternatives from the receptor society. This echoes to some extent Brah's repudiations of rather essentialized descriptions of diaspora space, and her preference for more constructivist notions that encompass their heterogeneous and, importantly, contested nature[6] — particularly relevant, we would add, to

---

[3] See Linda Basch, Nina Glick Schiller and Cristina Szanton Blanc, *Nations Unbound: Transnational Projects, Colonial Predicaments and Deterritorialized Nation-States* (Amsterdam: Gordon and Breach Science Publications, 1994) for the seminal framing of the transnational migration model.

[4] See Sheringham in this volume for an enlightening discussion of such critiques and the notion of transnational social spaces from a geopolitical perspective. Also see Richard Alba and Victor Nee, 'Rethinking Assimilation Theory for a New Era of Immigration', *International Migration Review*, 31, 4 (1997), 826–74; Rogers Brubacker, 'The Return of Assimilation? Changing Perspective on Immigration and its Sequels in France, Germany and the United States', *Ethnic and Racial Studies*, 24, 4 (2001), 531–48; Peter Kivisto, *Incorporating Diversity: Rethinking Assimilation in a Multicultural Age* (Boulder, CO: Paradigm, 2005); and Ewa Morawska, 'In Defense of the Assimilation Model', *Journal of American Ethnic History*, 13, 2 (1994), 76–87.

[5] Alejandro Portes, Luis E. Guarnizo and Patricia Landolt, 'The Study of Transnationalism: Pitfalls and Promise of an Emergent Research', *Ethnic and Racial Studies*, 22, 2 (1999), 217–37.

[6] Avtar Brah, *Cartographies of Diaspora: Contesting Identities* (London: Routledge, 1996), pp. 181–84.

transnational scenarios. Furthermore, such processes are bi-directional, since the migrants' presence in a given society also influences its sociocultural fabric, not only in terms of visibility and mobilization of resources but also in terms of cultural possibility for the receptor population.

One final concept important to our discussion of transnational lives is Hall's delineation of 'becoming' with regards to identity.[7] Key is the idea mooted above, that migrants negotiate heterogeneous, diverse identities and allegiances that are not fixed or enduring, intrinsic or predetermined. Therefore, complex and multiple identities are the norm and can be constructed, assumed or abandoned as required, for they differ in their relative significance and import.[8] The malleability of identity becomes evident, for example, when migrant groups emphasize the social and political usefulness of a collective ethnic identity and its instrumental mobilization to particular ends. In this way, loyalties to particular identification strategies are not necessarily divided, since inherent and 'borrowed' qualities and traits are not mutually exclusive.

Methodology

A combined methodology was used in this study, including ethnographic observations of day-to-day life social and cultural practices (e.g. attendance at Catholic mass, coffee gatherings, school activities), participant-observation at specific events (football matches, religious and cultural festivals) and associational activities of Spanish and Portuguese local clubs and societies, such as *o Clube Português* and the Hispanic Society of Southampton. We have termed these social and cultural fields 'visible platforms of Spanish and Portuguese ethnicities'. It was through these interfaces that we were able to identify and interview key gatekeepers and community leaders who provided us with intra-group interpretations of migration histories and trajectories, and an analysis of their current situation, aspirations and challenges.[9] Whenever possible, our observations were closely aligned across the two migrant groups in order to maintain a comparative perspective. When this was not feasible, we drew on archival documents and

[7] Stuart Hall, 'Politics of Identity', in *Culture, Identity and Politics: Ethnic Minorities in Britain*, ed. by Terence Ranger (Aldershot: Avebury, 1991), pp. 129–35; 'Cultural Identity and Diaspora', in *Theorizing Diaspora*, ed. by Jana Evans Braziel and Anita Mannur (Oxford: Blackwell, 2003), pp. 233–46.

[8] *Ethnic Groups and Boundaries: The Social Organisation of Cultural Difference*, ed. by Fredrik Barth (Oslo: Universitetsforlaget, 1969); 'Enduring and Emerging Issues in the Analysis of Ethnicity', in *The Anthropology of Ethnicity: Beyond Groups and Boundaries*, ed. by Hans Vermeulen and Cora Govers (Amsterdam: Het Spinhuis, 1994), pp. 11–32.

[9] We understand gatekeepers to be individuals who occupy a prominent position in the social and cultural settings under study, which allows them to control access to information and participants or to act as cultural brokers, such as community leaders, interpreters, event organizers and leaders of migrant associations. In the course of this research the key gatekeepers had leading roles in the visible platforms delineated above. Inevitably, the choice of gatekeepers has a significant impact in shaping the research but their involvement was crucial in order to gain access to and trust amongst migrants.

secondary sources that enabled us to document and gain a fuller picture of the longitudinal patterns of settlement and incorporation of the groups.

We should clarify at this point our use of the terms 'ethnicity' and 'community', since in the context of this paper their connotations are strongly interlinked. As Sheringham points out in her essay on Brazilian migration in Gort, the term 'community' is often somewhat problematic, since its use generally implies a homogeneous, unified, cohesive body or group of people. We also recognize the implications of using the term 'ethnicity' in a similar way, that is, as representative of a homogeneous, uniform term to encompass national characteristics, as Mar-Molinero avers in her essay on Madeirans on Jersey. Nonetheless, our aim in this essay is to demonstrate that both terms can be applied to the Portuguese in Bournemouth. For many migrant groups, a visible sociocultural and sociolinguistic presence within the receptor society, and the performance within their daily lives of customs and activities commonly practised in the home nation, may serve as a way to reinforce a sense of community and ethnic affiliation, even if not all individuals share all customs etc. in their local contexts, and even if the traits highlighted correspond to language use and cultural pursuits that may well be seen as essentially formulaic by younger migrants and by other social strata. Thus, it is the shared experiences, common attachments and bonds and sense of communion between individuals coming from one nation that may serve to create an impression of community.[10] We will also consider the notions of symbolic community with relation to the Spanish, whereby ethnic artefacts are recalled as a way of recreating a shared sense of Spanish ethnicity, again irrespective of the differing local (home) contexts of the migrants in question.

Results and Discussion

We now focus on the different levels of visibility of each group and on the configuration of their current geocultural anchoring across Bournemouth and surrounding areas, considering language use as a sociocultural practice and potential carrier of self-identification practices.

The Portuguese migratory patterns that occurred in the period under consideration were generally characterized by the movement of individuals or very small groups in search of economic stability and security, as we have intimated above. Most of the Portuguese migrants interviewed came from Madeira or northern Portugal. In the Spanish case however, there was not only a wider diversity of origins, including Galicia, Andalusia, Catalonia and Valencia, but also of alleged motivations for migration, which included: economic reasons, political considerations, perception of better employment and professional opportunities in the UK, embarking on higher education courses, and the desire to learn English.

From the initial phases of migration and settlement in the 1970s and 1980s, Portuguese insertion is shaped by a multicultural model. Unlike the Spanish

---

[10] See in this context Benedict Anderson, *Imagined Communities: Reflection on the Origins and Spread of Nationalism*, rev. edn (London and New York: Verso, 1991).

case studies that we present below, the Portuguese migrants that we interviewed appear to identify as a community distinct from that of the overarching society, as the following fieldwork citations demonstrates:

> Quem somos? Muitos de vós já nos conhecem, já comemoramos juntos, já nos reunimos, mas para quem não nos conhece, somos um grupo de pessoas honestas que decidiram juntar esforços para o bem da *comunidade* portuguesa.[11]
>
> [Who are we? Many of you already know who we are, we've already celebrated events together, we've had meetings together, but for those who don't know us, we are a group of honest people who have decided to join forces for the good of the Portuguese *community*.]
>
> E nós emigrantes, como unidade fazemos os nossos pequenos business [...].[12]
>
> [And we emigrants, between us, we have our own small businesses [...].]

Often, as we have stated above, the use of 'community' encompasses a degree of physical or textual visibility and material traceability within the linguistic landscape, 'the language of public road signs, advertising billboards, street names, commercial shop signs, and public signs on government buildings combines to form the linguistic landscape of a given territory, region, or urban agglomeration'.[13] Thus, within a well-defined geographical space, visible platforms of migrant presence and socio-economic and sociocultural practices may become representative of their ethnicity. For the Portuguese this is manifest partially through their urban clustering around one particular neighbourhood of Bournemouth known as 'the Triangle', and to a lesser extent in the more outlying district of Boscombe. The Triangle appears to be the first point of arrival not only for Portuguese newcomers but also for migrants of other nationalities. It is an area of inexpensive hotels and bed and breakfast establishments that offers service sector work in the tourist industry, as well as cheap accommodation to these migrants, just as it did to Spanish migrants when they first arrived in the 1960s and 1970s. Over time, the Portuguese have emphasized their physical presence in this area through commercial outlets, e.g. bars, shops, cafes and restaurants with overtly Portuguese names, reference and foodstuffs, which serve to highlight rather than conceal their ethnic grouping, for example, the restaurants 'Funchal By Night' and 'Atlântico'. The majority of these establishments are aimed at providing services to the Portuguese themselves, rather than introducing elements of Portuguese culture to the tourist trade in Bournemouth. Similarly, there have been attempts to set up sociocultural associations such as the *Clube Português*:

> O objectivo da associação é cumprir e [...] promover a cultura portuguesa dentro da comunidade, especialmente para os filhos [...] não esquecer a

---

[11] *Boletim Informativo Do Clube Português*, Edição 1, Junho 2006, p. 2 [our emphasis].

[12] Interview with C., male Portuguese community gatekeeper, Bournemouth, 30 February 2006.

[13] Rodrigue Bourhis and Richard Landry, 'Linguistic Landscape and Ethnolinguistic Vitality: An Empirical Study', *Journal of Language and Social Psychology*, 16, 1 (1997), 23–49.

sua cultura, onde as pessoas têm a opção de saber o que é ser português. [...] Queremos acabar com a *poverty*, a pobreza na comunidade portuguesa. Queremos pôr a comunidade como força de trabalho que sempre existiu.[14]

[The aim of our association is to maintain and [...] promote Portuguese culture within the community, above all so that our children [...] do not forget their cultural heritage, [and] where people can really find out what being Portuguese means [...]. We want to put an end to poverty within the Portuguese community. We want to turn the community back into the strong workforce that it once was.]

Indeed, there is a strong belief that their definition of 'Portuguese culture' should be preserved, and a special emphasis is placed on particular community events and gatherings, such as the family excursion that was organized to attend the festivities of the *Dia de Portugal* in London.[15] In the words of one of the community leaders interviewed, the aim of this outing was 'to teach the children what it means to be *um português na Inglaterra*'.[16] There have also been attempts to set up *Associações de Pais* in order to mobilize language and education resources for the children of migrants; for example, some funding for special language staff at the local primary school has been secured in recent years.

Such initiatives lend some credence to the use of the term 'Portuguese community' by gatekeepers and cultural brokers, a community which they articulate as being in the process of becoming 'organized'. 'Organization' here is expressed in sociopolitical terms, as it refers to the processes of creating self-help structures and enabling mobilization of institutional resources within the receptor society or even by the home country:

A missão do Clube (Português) está para ajudar aos portugueses para se ajudarem a si mesmo. Pede à própria comunidade que crie trabalho, aos portugueses que já são managers, outros são chefes, e que dão oportunidades aos outros. Se a gente precisar transporte de alguém, ou dar uma cama ou dar abrigo a alguém, as pessoas vem nos dar à gente da comunidade [...].[17]

[The mission of the Portuguese Club is to help the Portuguese learn how to help themselves. It asks their own community — the Portuguese who are managers and owners of businessess — to create jobs, to furnish work opportunities for others. If we need help with transport, or need to offer someone a bed or shelter for the night, then these people are there to help us, the community.]

Indeed, the local authorities have started to make provision for some of the specific needs of the Portuguese in Bournemouth. Social services now provide both statutory and voluntary community services and engage interpreters and mediators to assist with language issues, particularly in dealings with the police

[14] Interview with C., Bournemouth, 22 February 2006.
[15] '*Excursão familiar, 11 de Junho de 2006: Dia de Portugal, de Camões e das Comunidades Portuguesas*'. Poster information distributed at the Portuguese *Café Europa* in Boscombe, advertising the annual event held in Kennington Park, London.
[16] Interview with C., Bournemouth, 22 February 2006.
[17] Interview with C., Bournemouth, 30 February 2006.

and magistrate's courts. This focus on interactions with the justice system is an issue of concern for the gatekeepers interviewed, since they believe that it simply lends credence to the idea that a largely conflictual relationship exists with the receptor society, with migrants being portrayed by the receptor society as 'needy', 'exploited' and 'non-assimilated'. In contrast, the gatekeepers' own narration of the Portuguese community often refers to attempts it makes to overcome problems which, from the migrant perspective, relate to integration and which often arise from a misunderstanding, on both sides, of different cultural contexts, norms and expectations. This is indicated in the following citation from an interview with B, another Portuguese community gatekeeper, who refers to children's perceived behaviour in school:

> Estamos a falar de 1998: não há muito tempo; o meu filho foi posto várias vezes de castigo. Não podia jogar com os outros miúdos a bola. O problema maior era a língua. Como não eram percebidos eram postos de parte. Como não conseguiam explicar eram castigados. Quem é que começa a luta? Podia ser o português ou podia ser o inglês. Mas, como o português não conseguia explicar, eram postos de castigo.[18]

> [We are talking about 1998: not long ago; my son was disciplined several times. He wasn't allowed to play ball with the other kids. The main issue was language; because they were not understood they were segregated, and because they couldn't explain [what happened] they were punished. Who started the fight? It could have been the Portuguese boy or it could have been the English boy, but since the Portuguese boy couldn't explain what happened, he was punished.]

Recently, the area of Boscombe in Bournemouth has started to emerge as a type of 'buffer' or transition zone for some of the Portuguese. Movement away from the inner-city neighbourhoods seems to coincide with a certain desire for upward mobility and distance from the idea of a Portuguese community, something that, incidentally, was also reflected in C's earlier quote. Another respondent explained that privacy had become paramount for her family, something that 'is not possible to maintain in the Triangle, where everybody knows about everybody's business'.[19] Similarly, this respondent explained how she would like her family to be able 'to live like the rest of the people in the receptor society', something that she is pursuing by means of putting some physical distance between her family and the rest of the Portuguese community. As we explain later, such overt aspirations for immersion and integration within the receptor society appear to echo those expressed by Spanish migrants who have settled permanently in the UK. However, we will return to the impact of such aspirations on language use for these families later.

Spanish migrants arriving in Bournemouth did not usually envisage permanent settlement, and the initial focus of those who came seeking work was to amass savings, gain skills in the workplace or improve their education in a way that

---

[18] Interview with B, female Portuguese community gatekeeper, Bournemouth, 17 March 2006.
[19] Informal conversation with F, female Portuguese migrant, in *Café Europa*, 22 February 2006.

would be of benefit once they returned to Spain. However, as many migrants married and started families, this idea of return very quickly became a delayed horizon rather than an immediate reality: what was envisaged as short-term migration gradually became more definitive, particularly, but not exclusively, in the case of those migrants who married English men or women. During the 1960s and 1970s, influenced largely by the hitherto dominant assimilationist paradigm, these Spaniards gradually became inserted into British society. However, for the Spanish migrants interviewed in this project, this integration was not contentious. Rather, it was both actively desired and explicitly carried out. These respondents avow recognition that changes in their familial circumstances entailed a reorientation of their goals and aspirations. In many cases they firmly believe that in the long term they have achieved a high level of identification with British society. Many even cite the advantages of being the only Spaniard in certain British social or cultural contexts as a factor that facilitated their integration and acceptance into the receptor society, and this is further encapsulated by comments concerning invisibility and being almost indistinguishable from members of this receptor society. Thus, in their narratives they deny belonging to a Spanish ethnic 'community' in the UK and go so far as to reject the notion of community outright, even for other ethnicities:

> Pienso que cuando vas a otro país, por ejemplo, cuando los indios vienen aquí y por las circunstancias que sean permanecen en un círculo indio en Birmingham o donde sea, eso es malísimo porque ¿cómo puedes ser indio en Gran Bretaña, amigo mío? Puedes serlo en la India pero no puedes esperar ser indio aquí y operar con normalidad. Si has de funcionar normalmente, mi conclusión es que si emigras y es una cosa temporal se te puede perdonar, pero si te vas a quedar mucho tiempo tienes que intentar integrarte lo más posible, no simplemente acomodarte.[20]

> [I think that when you go to another country, for instance, when Indians come over here and for whatever reason they remain within an Indian circle in Birmingham or wherever, well that is terrible, because, how can you be Indian in Britain, my friend? You can be in India but you cannot expect to be it here and behave as normal. If you simply have to behave the way is normal for you, my view that if you emigrate and it is something temporary you can be forgiven, but if you're going to stay for a long time you have to try to integrate as much as possible, not just accommodate.]

In addition, these respondents rarely self-identify as 'migrants' since they perceive this a problematic category, and often they stress the uniqueness of their life experiences, rather than their arrival in the UK as part of a migration flow or system,[21] as the following respondent illustrates:

> No, no, no, no, yo no soy un emigrante. Yo me considero un señor que estaba trabajando allí en España y que conoció a una mujer, se enamoró y se vino

[20] Interview with R., Spanish male member of the Hispanic Society of Southampton, Winchester, 19 February 2002.
[21] See in this context Kathleen Paul, *Whitewashing Britain: Race and Citizenship in the Postwar Era* (Ithaca, NY: Cornell University Press, 1997).

aquí. De emigrante nada. Yo he venido a este país a traer dinero y me traje dinero de España para acá. Que el emigrante se viene sin nada. Yo siempre he pagado mis impuestos y siempre he pagado al gobierno. Nunca. Yo tuve la suerte de que no tenía que emigrar, no lo necesitaba, fue por aventura.[22]

[No, no, no, no, I'm not a migrant. I consider myself a man who was working in Spain and met his [British] wife there, fell in love and came over here. I'm not an emigrant at all. I've come to this country with money and I brought money from Spain. Because migrants come with nothing. I've always paid my taxes and the government. No, not a migrant. I was lucky that I didn't have to emigrate, I didn't need to, it was simply an adventure.]

If and when the term 'migration' is used by Spanish respondents about themselves, and the issue discussed in any detail, it is always done with historical distance. In their interviews, Spaniards refer to *'la gran emigración de los años 60'* as a historical construct, considered now to be a finished, closed migration flow, even though its time period frames their own arrival in the country.

Moreover, the Spaniards are not constitutive of a migrant community in terms of a well-defined demarcation of geographical space or ethnic clustering. Indeed, their geographical anchoring appears to be indistinguishable from that of their British receptors. Not only in Bournemouth, but also in other locations in the south where they settled e.g. Dorchester, Southampton and Winchester, there are no particular areas or neighbourhoods of Spanish population presence,[23] unlike the Portuguese referred to earlier. Thus, these respondents demonstrate little visible socio-economic materiality within their surrounding linguistic landscape. The few Spanish restaurants that exist in the areas under study were found to be mostly conceived as profitable commercial outlets, aimed at a wider British market rather than at an ethnic one.

Furthermore, in Bournemouth little visible sociocultural materiality exists in the form of associations and cultural events, such as 'ethnic' festivals or migrant support networks. Instead, the Spanish/Hispanic associations that our search for visible platforms of Spanish ethnicity revealed, for instance, the Hispanic Society of Southampton, were found to have as their primary aim the promotion of the Spanish language and culture, not so much with a preservation agenda in mind, but guided by the perception that they constitute a valuable and fashionable cultural capital that can be shared with the British. It is interesting to note that many Spanish and Hispanic Societies across the UK were originally established to assist migrants when they first arrived in the UK, but have, over time, evolved into essentially cultural societies, even though they sometimes appear listed in public directories and websites of an 'ethnic community' nature.[24]

---

[22] Interview with M., Spanish male bar owner, Bournemouth, 30 May 2002.

[23] This is not the case in London, where there are visible institutional traces of a denser concentration of Spanish migrants e.g. around Portobello and Camden Town, primarily due to lower housing costs.

[24] However, in London some Spanish associations and institutions still revolve around the preservation and transmission of the Spanish language and culture, e.g. the *Centro Social de Mayores*. For an analysis of Spanish migrant associations in the UK, refer to Alicia Pozo-

Language as a Social-Cultural Practice

In mapping out the linguistic trajectory of the Spanish migrants, there appear to be three key stages that account for the loss and recovery of the mother tongue; firstly, arrival and settlement, secondly, a mid-term period of starting and raising families and finally, long-term retrospection and reflection about their migration experiences. We now discuss how migrants' linguistic practices clearly highlight the tensions surrounding the juxtaposition of these stages, which, as we stated above are subject to constant and continual appraisal and evaluation.

Traditional 'one nation, one language, one state' ideologies, such as those which abounded in nineteenth-century nationalist philosophy, are often somewhat fictive and artificial constructs, as Barbour points out, and tend to be based on idealized monocultural and monolingual notions of political and societal structure.[25] Such ideologies have endorsed the concept of a homogeneous national identity that would subsume alternative ethnic or 'national' identities and their associated cultures and languages — through assimilation processes outlined earlier in this paper — since the very existence of unassimilated minoritized groups or 'nations' within the framework of the larger one was seen as leading to a complete or partial disintegration of the overriding 'one nation, one language, one state' configuration.[26]

At the time of the Spanish informants' initial stage of migration and settlement, this association of a national identity with majority language monolingualism and cultural homogeneity was pervasive in British society. As a result, there ensued a tension between the maintenance of Spanish as the mother tongue and the acquisition of English, learnt as the functional language within the receptor society. In accordance with Joseph's reflections regarding the linguistic aspects of identification and how they interact with the observable roles of language in context,[27] we would contend that the desire to identify with the overarching society resulted in a general shift away from the use of Spanish in contexts other than explicitly intra-group ones (e.g. visits and vacations in Spain, or phone calls and letters to Spanish relatives).

Gutiérrez, Doc 1/2005 'Emigración española en Inglaterra: prácticas asociativas, integración e identidad (Madrid: Fundación 1 de Mayo, 2005); online at <http://www2.1mayo.ccoo.es/publicaciones/doctrab/doc205.pdf> [accessed 12 November 2009].

[25] Stephen Barbour, 'Language, Nationalism, Europe', in *Language and Nationalism in Europe*, ed. by Stephen Barbour and Cathie Carmichael (Oxford: Oxford University Press, 2000), pp. 1–17 (p. 4).

[26] For further discussion, see Jaine Beswick, *Regional Nationalism in Spain: Language Use and Ethnic Identity in Galicia* (Clevedon: Multilingual Matters, 2007), pp. 28–32; John Gibbons and Elizabeth Ramírez, *Maintaining a Minority Language: A Case Study of Hispanic Teenagers* (Clevedon: Multilingual Matters, 2004), p. 191; Tove Skutnabb-Kangas, *Linguistic Genocide in Education: Or Worldwide Diversity and Human Rights?* (London: Lawrence Erlbaum Associates 2000), p. 426.

[27] John Earl Joseph, *Language and Identity: National, Ethnic, Religious* (Basingstoke: Palgrave Macmillan, 2004), p. 11.

The second stage, that of starting a family within a British context, was for many migrants an important milestone in their migratory trajectories, as the expectation of return to Spain one day now became subject to renegotiation. Acceptance of the fact that the socialization and education of children implied a degree of permanence in the receptor society also started to generate a new set of behavioural patterns involving language choice, use and transmission. As Pozo-Gutiérrez highlights in her earlier paper,[28] behaviour patterns were now subject not only to individuals' attitudes and behaviours in the private sphere, but also to external constraints, and to institutional and political factors. The 1970s British education system was characterized by a monolingual, monocultural, essentially assimilationist curriculum, in which English was the sole language of instruction, which discouraged autochthonous language maintenance in favour of receptor society language shift. Whereas initially English had tended to be acquired for inter-group communications, the entry of Spanish migrants' children into the mainstream school system often resulted in an acceleration of family and intra-group language shift to English, with the consequent loss of Spanish as the mother tongue. Once a reasonable level of fluency in English was achieved, this, in turn, often resulted in an acceleration of social and cultural integration and a general consolidation of settlement patterns, something that we have not yet observed with regards to the Portuguese case, as we will explain below.

As an interesting counterpoint to the degree of integration witnessed, the general Spanish migratory patterns emerging from our interviews are now entering a third stage, that of reflection and retrospection, and of rediscovery and revival of ethnic, cultural, historical, political and linguistic roots. In the receptor society context, this has been fuelled largely by the emerging prestige and popularity of Hispanic culture — perceived, for instance, as being a successful source of cultural production e.g. film, music and dance — as well as nascent interest in learning the Spanish language. Our research not only confirms the findings of earlier research, which demonstrated that knowing Spanish has become fashionable with young people in general,[29] but it also indicates that this hispanization of popular culture is also encouraging the grandchildren of our informants to either learn Spanish for the first time, or to improve their competencies in it. By revisiting this facet of their heritage, some members of what we may term the 'third generation' are thus

---

[28] Alicia Pozo-Gutiérrez, 'From Neglect to Re-Discovery: Language and Identity amongst Spanish Migrants in the United Kingdom,' *International Journal of Iberian Studies* 19, 3 (2006), 205–30. At EU level, policies regarding multicultural models of education were debated in the late 1970s, but they were not formulated as directives until the early 1980s, too late to benefit the children of Spaniards involved in this paper.

[29] Cristina Mateo, 'Identities at a Distance: Markers of National Identity in the Video-Diaries of Second-Generation Spanish Migrants in London', in *Constructing Identity in Contemporary Spain: Theoretical Debates and Cultural Practice*, ed. by Jo Labanyi (Oxford: Oxford University Press, 2002), pp. 72–85. See also Jaine Beswick, 'Galician-Spanish-British? Migrant Identity in Guildford, UK', in *Galician Cultural Studies between the Local and the Global*, ed. by Kirsty Hooper and Manuel Puga Moruxa (London: MLA, in press 2010).

reconstructing what was largely a redundant linguistic identification strategy, and it may well be that the Spanish language is once again acquiring a degree of prestige as an identifier of group differentiation, and is further acquiring such prestige as a method of promoting a general cultural heritage within the receptor society itself, in line with constructivist hypotheses and Hall's notion of 'becoming'.

There also appear to be three key stages that map out the linguistic trajectory of the Portuguese in Bournemouth, broadly in line with the Spanish migratory patterns outlined above, although these account for the general maintenance of the mother tongue by the Portuguese rather than its loss and recovery. Firstly, we term the initial arrival stage as one of non-settlement; secondly, there is a mid-term stage when families were reunited in the UK; and thirdly, a tentative stage of transnational enactment. We will now discuss these stages and their relevance to the language practices of the Portuguese.

During the Portuguese informants' initial stage of migration, the association of a national identity with majority language monolingualism and cultural homogeneity pervaded British society, as it did for the Spanish. However, in line with the findings of previous research with the Portuguese on Jersey,[30] these migrants tended to maintain their autochthonous language, at the very least for intra-group communication, and made no concerted effort to learn English, the functional language within the receptor society. One respondent insisted that:

[o] português é a língua da casa; lá fora, pode-se falar o que quiser![31]

[Portuguese is the language of the home; outside you can speak whatever you like!]

Like many Spaniards, when they arrived in Bournemouth the 1960s, the Portuguese tended to stay in the same hostels and boarding houses clustered around the Triangle area of Bournemouth, in which their sociocultural and socio-economic needs were satisfied by the establishment of Portuguese shops and cafes, as we intimated earlier. The jobs they held at this time were mostly in the service sector, and very often there was little if any interaction with English-speaking employers, since work was generally found as a result of being 'a friend of a friend', as our earlier citations exemplified. Indeed, most work colleagues were also Portuguese, and as a result the majority of these migrants rarely acquired more than a few words of English. So in pragmatic terms, at the stage of arrival there was no strong need for these migrants to learn English in order to find work, housing, etc, and no reason for them to learn the language in order to be able to communicate with colleagues or in the area surrounding their homes. Furthermore, the maintenance of Portuguese as the intra-group language was

[30] Jaine Beswick, 'The Portuguese Diaspora in Jersey', in *The Consequences of Mobility: Linguistic and Sociocultural Contact Zones*, ed. by Bent Preisler, Anne Fabricius, Hartmut Haberland, Susanne Kjaerbeck and Karen Risager (Roskilde, Denmark: Roskilde University, 2005), online at <http://www.ruc.dk/cuid/publikationer/publikationer/mobility/mobility2/Beswick/> [accessed 30 November 2009].
[31] Interview with P., Portuguese male, Bournemouth, 4 May 2007.

essential to the notions of returning one day to the Portuguese homeland:

> Epá, para muitos portugueses não valia a pena aprender o inglês; quase todos queriam voltar um dia para a ilha [de Madeira].[32]
>
> [Well, for many Portuguese there was no point in learning English; almost everyone wanted to go back to the Island one day.]
>
> A dinâmica migratória, a mentalidade de imigração é só imigrar para comprar a sua casinha [...] regressar a Portugal 10 ou 15 anos depois [...].[33]
>
> [The driving force behind migration, the migratory mentality is that you migrate only until you can buy your own house [...] and then return to Portugal 10 or 15 years later [...].]

This, then, was a period of 'non-settlement': the retention of Portuguese safeguarded and would thus facilitate the migrants' potential for future re-integration into Madeiran society. It highlighted the temporary nature of their stay in Bournemouth and reinforced their reluctance to identify linguistically with the overarching receptor society, or to integrate into it in any significant way. Language use was thus central to the identification strategies of these migrants.

The second, 'mid-term' stage appears to have begun in the 1980s, once migrants sent for their children, many of whom had stayed on Madeira or in mainland Portugal with their extended families until the parents could find regular work. In the Triangle, many of these Portuguese children heard little if any English before school age, given that very often they were somewhat 'cocooned' within a network of multiple Portuguese families living together and sharing the burden of continuous childcare, especially when both parents worked long or unsociable hours. Therefore, the transition from Portuguese to English as the language of use in the local primary school was problematic, and as one respondent asserts, the lack of English often incited bullying:

> [...] quando eles foram para a escola, eles vinham a chorar todos os dias [...]. Chegavam a casa e diziam que eram mal tratados e que os outros meninos os tratavam mal. E que não os percebiam, é que eles não eram percebidos.[34]
>
> [When they went to school, they would cry every day [...]. They would get home and say that they were badly treated and that the other children were horrible to them. They didn't understand them; the point was that they were not understood.]

Yet at home there was little parental support for, or acceptance of, the need of the children to learn English in order to be able to cope at school. Unlike the Spanish case, during the 1980s and 1990s, the English educational context did not generate a new set of behavioural patterns among the Portuguese, and there was no significant parental and hence, family, language shift to English:

---

[32] Interview with J., Portuguese female, Bournemouth, 4 May 2007.
[33] Interview with C., Bournemouth, 22 February 2006.
[34] Interview with B., 17 March 2006.

[...] o problema maior era os pais não saberem inglês.[35]

[The main problem was that the parents did not know any English.]

More recently, return expectations have become subject to renegotiation and appraisal for some of our Portuguese respondents, who appear resigned to staying in Bournemouth longer than originally planned. This is due in no small part to their tacit acceptance that even under a recession, their work opportunities are better in the UK than in Portugal, and this resembles the context of resignation to non-return of many Spanish migrants following the international economic crisis of the mid 1970s. Yet many adult Portuguese have little, if any, English, and still rely on mediation support from community leaders and gatekeepers. Interestingly, however, parents now consider the children's acquisition of English at school as a potential resource, not only for their children, but also for themselves. In situations which require contact with the receptor society, children are often required to act as interpreters for their parents, particularly in daily, routine scenarios such as at the doctor's surgery or at the benefits' office.[36] Some parents now even discourage their children from speaking Portuguese to each other outside the home, and refuse to let them take the language classes funded by the Portuguese government at the local primary school. Although Portuguese still remains a core value of Portuguese identity and group differentiation within the confines of their discrete ethnic community, some members are starting to acknowledge the usefulness of English language learning for their children and, by analogy, for them. However, this appears to be a strictly pragmatic application, since strong relationships are still not established with the receptor community through this use of English, and as the following citation demonstrates, some respondents still see integration as a problem:

o problema da segunda geração quando chegar a altura de regressar os nos filhos já se adaptaram [...].[37]

[The problem with the second generation is that when it comes to the time of return, the children have already started to adapt [to the receptor culture] [...].]

Nonetheless, transnational aspirations do appear to permeate what may be a further stage of the linguistic trajectory of the Portuguese in Bournemouth, which demonstrates the potential fluidity of migratory relationships. A few Portuguese families have recently moved out of the Triangle area and into Boscombe and other outlying areas, as discussed earlier, and have a clearly stated aim of wanting to become more geoculturally dispersed amongst the receptor society at the same time as retaining and actively contributing to the construction of a strong sense of Portuguese community. The acquisition of English by the whole family enhances their relationship with the receptor society and offers

---

[35] Interview with B., 17 March 2006.
[36] The issue of multilingual education in this context will be discussed further in a forthcoming paper.
[37] Interview with C., 30 February 2006.

them a way of integrating:

> Os pais ficam contentes que os filhos sabem falar as duas línguas [...].[38]
>
> [Parents are happy that their children know the two languages [...].]

In keeping with aspirations for social mobility, another way that these migrants strengthen their ties with the receptor society is through initiatives to improve prospective work and educational opportunities, as the following responses from C. and B. illustrate:

> Fomos ao Town Hall, organizámos uma cosmopolitan business association [...] foi organizada com a colaboração do Town Hall, Businesslink, o chefe da polícia, pelo college e várias [...]. Houve entrevistas e o council tá muito interessado em apoiar a comunidade portuguesa [...].[39]
>
> [We went to the Town Hall, we organized a cosmopolitan business association [...] it was organized with the collaboration of the Town Hall, Businesslink, the police chief, the college and others [...]. There were interviews and the Council is very interested in supporting the Portuguese community [...].]
>
> É um projecto que vai começar agora. Vai dar formação profissional às pessoas. Só depois as pessoas terem formação profissional, primeiro o inglês. Foi logo o que eu diz, aqui o que nós precisamos é em primeiro lugar o inglês, depois poderem dar a formação profissional. Portanto isto é um plano para cinco anos. Se a comunidade portuguesa não estiver interessada, nós estamos fora mas era bom porque eu sei que há muitas pessoas que poderiam deixar de limpar quartos. Por exemplo, de ganhar 4 libras a hora e passar a ganhar 6, 7, 8.[40]
>
> [It is a project that's about to start. It will give professional training to people. But only after they've learnt English. This was what I said; [that] here what we need in the first place is English, and only then professional training. However, this is a five-year plan. If the Portuguese community shows no interest, we will be out of it, but it would be good to do because I know that there are many people who then could stop being cleaners; they could go from earning £4 an hour to earning £6, £7 or £8 for example.]

It may well be that in certain quarters notions of return are beginning to coexist with an aspirational framework of opportunity and self-development that inevitably prolongs the commitment of migrants to the receptor society. At the same time however, these migrants affirm a committed desire to maintain Portuguese in intra-group contexts, and particularly in domestic scenarios, even though return to Portugal no longer always appears to be their ultimate goal. Indeed, these informants do not consider their use of both languages and the acquisition and maintenance of sociocultural norms, to be mutually exclusive.

---

[38] Interview with S., Brazilian female language assistant at local primary school, 4 May 2007.
[39] Interview with C., 30 February 2006. The event referred to is the *Encontro Cosmopolita de Negociantes da Comunidade* that took place on 9 May 2006 at the Pavilion Theatre in Bournemouth. From the details that appeared on the Portuguese version of the agenda, the aim of the event was to brief representatives of different local migrant communities on the support services available to set up in business.
[40] Interview with B., 17 March 2007.

Conclusions

At the time of their arrival, and during the first phases of settlement, the Spaniards who came to the UK in the 1960s often engaged in similar associational practices as some Portuguese in Bournemouth engage in now, in order to overcome initial difficulties and facilitate their initial insertion in Britain, e.g. in terms of employment, education, rights, etc. However, in doing so, they did not aspire to being perceived as an ethnic group. Indeed, they tried to actively integrate at the very least at linguistic, occupational and educational levels, evidenced by the sociocultural trajectories of many of our Spanish respondents. Even those whose limited competencies in English restrict their aspirations for integration, their interviews and oral histories convey their desire to become indistinguishable from the autochthonous population and not to be seen as part of a 'self-segregated' migrant community of multicultural Britain.

However, this has not entailed a total disappearance of Spanish social and cultural practices if we are to judge by the current re-attachment to and re-discovery of Spanish 'culture', whatever forms this takes. In the case of the activities of the Hispanic Society of Southampton, for instance, this would be a somewhat contrived celebration of all things Spanish in a British context through, for example, monthly talks on Spanish topics.

Gan's early concept of 'symbolic ethnicity',[41] often employed in the analysis of identity negotiation amongst contemporary ethnic groups, is useful in the framing of this revival of Spanish ethno-cultural practices and may also enable us speculate about the evolution of Portuguese sociocultural and sociolinguistic practices. Symbolic ethnicity entails a range of strategies associated with ethnic and religious (and we would add, linguistic) identity negotiation. Gans argues that ethnic cultures do not experience the straight-line assimilation proposed by the melting-pot principle. Instead, they respond to social pressures of behaviour in which ethnic identities are maintained on an idiosyncratic basis, helping to mitigate the social and psychological upheaval experienced by migrants in their receptor environments. The model also describes the importance of nostalgia and sentiments to identity negotiation (as opposed to rigorous adherence to the culture of origin).

The Portuguese appear to form a distinct community in the areas that we have researched. Their presence is articulated in a 'problematic' way — as migrants who struggle to integrate, who need resources, and who do not speak the language. Nevertheless, there is already some evidence that some members are beginning to aspire to that 'indistinction' that the Spaniards themselves pursued as a strategy to become successfully integrated. In this respect, 'social class' emerges as a key variable, not only in terms of belonging to particular social strata at the time of arrival, but more importantly, in terms of aspiration. The Portuguese who have left 'Little Lisbon' (as the Triangle is known) want to start businesses, and some

---

[41] Herbert Gans, 'Symbolic Ethnicity: The Future of Ethnic Groups and Cultures in America', *Ethnic and Racial Studies*, 2, 1 (1979), 1–20.

have children who have claimed a British as well as a Portuguese identification, and who are considering their settlement in the UK as something long-term or even permanent. Despite the efforts made by community leaders to organize the community around a cultural association, there are signs that the Portuguese are not taking part in sufficient numbers to justify these efforts. In many cases they are too busy working. In others, they are just not interested.

It remains to be seen whether the Portuguese follow the same journey as the Spanish have done since their arrival in Britain, with their cultural practices becoming essentialized along similar lines and eventually turning into something symbolic, capitalized on by both the British and the migrants themselves. There are some signs that this is beginning to happen. One of the main Portuguese restaurants in Bournemouth is no longer frequented by the local Portuguese community, but has turned into an expensive and fashionable restaurant aimed at a wider audience. The Spanish case could be seen in some respects as a model to predict the possible trajectory that the Portuguese community might follow, which, if proven, may entail its gradual disappearance.

The differentiation of a migrant group such as the Portuguese from others may also be expressed through linguistic practices, and a sense of solidarity and inclusiveness between members occurs if they share the same positive attitudes towards the use of their language as a core value of identity.[42] Language may thus become fundamental to the group's ethnicity and acquire prestige as an important identifier of the group's status and distinctiveness.[43]

We could argue that what we are witnessing in our research is pure pragmatism, where the need to fit in and to survive in an unfamiliar environment translates into the need to adapt to new cultural values and to diversify both 'customers' and audiences. This has already happened in the Spanish case, where essentialized and rediscovered cultural symbols are currently valued by migrants and the autochthonous population alike. In the Portuguese case, however, essentialized symbols are only valued within the group. These are the questions that will guide the second phase of our enquiry.

In mapping out the Spanish and Portuguese presence in this study, we initially came across two distinct migratory trajectories that, from a longitudinal perspective, appeared to be contextually convergent but theoretically divergent. Whilst the socio-economic and sociopolitical contexts that resulted in these migrations shared similar characteristics, the observed evolution, maintenance and migration dynamics of these groups seemed at first to differ. However, based on these initial findings, we conclude that the migration of the Spanish and Portuguese is not necessarily definitive as far as identification strategies are

---

[42] Jerzy Smolicz, 'In Search of a Multicultural Nation: The Case of Australia from an International Perspective', in *Cultural Democracy and Ethnic Pluralism: Multicultural and Multilingual Policies in Education*, ed. by Richard J. Watts and Jerzy J. Smolicz (Frankfurt: Peter Lang, 1997), pp. 52–76 (p. 67).
[43] Beswick, *Regional Nationalism in Spain*, pp. 37–41.

concerned, since immersion and long-term projection into the receptor society do not always imply full integration, nor do they always entail ethnic grouping. Rather, the Spanish and Portuguese migrants at the centre of this study appear to be positioned at some point along a continuum on which their patterns of accommodation into the receptor society vary regarding the time at which they occur and how the different sociolinguistic and sociocultural manifestations they produce.

We would like to thank all our respondents for the time and energy they put into interviews in the course of this research.

UNIVERSITY OF SOUTHAMPTON

A Transnational Space? Transnational Practices, Place-Based Identity and the Making of 'Home' among Brazilians in Gort, Ireland

OLIVIA SHERINGHAM

Introduction

While the movement of people, ideas, and materials is far from a new phenomenon, it is widely acknowledged among scholars that fundamental technological and demographic transformations have created accelerated, and potentially irreversible, forms of global interconnectedness. Such profound changes have, in many cases, challenged well-established paradigms within the study of migration, requiring new forms of theoretical analysis and new research methods.[1] Indeed, analyses of migration that pointed to linear movements from one nation state to another have increasingly been revealed as insufficient to describe realities in which migrants in fact have 'complex relations to different locales [...] involving social, symbolic and material ties between homelands, destinations and relations between destinations'.[2] This paper contributes to the study of these global shifts through an in-depth study of the migration experiences of a recent, yet very significant, Brazilian presence in the small Irish town of Gort, in county Galway. More specifically, through a focus on place, it explores the relationship between the transnational practices and the local attachment of Brazilian migrants in Gort.

The emergence of 'transnational studies' during the early 1990s, and widespread interest in 'diaspora' and 'diasporic studies', reflect responses to the analytical challenges created by the complex practices and relationships of individuals and communities living their lives across borders — both real and imaginary — or in places distant from their homelands.[3] A further response to

---

[1] Peggy Levitt, *The Transnational Villagers* (Berkeley: University of California Press, 2001).

[2] Floya Anthias, 'Metaphors of Home: Gendering New Migrations to Southern Europe', in *Gender and Migration in Southern Europe: Women on the Move*, ed. by Floya Anthias and Gabriella Lazaridis (Oxford: Berg, 2000), pp. 15–48 (pp. 21–22).

[3] For a discussion of the emergence of 'transnational studies', see Nina Glick-Schiller, 'Transnationality', in *A Companion to the Anthropology of Politics*, ed. by David Nugent and Joan Vincent (Oxford: Blackwell, 2004), pp. 448–67; Steven Vertovec, 'Conceiving and Researching Transnationalism,' *Ethnic and Racial Studies*, 22, 2 (1999), 447–62. For a discussion of the notion of 'diaspora' see Robin Cohen, *Global Diasporas: An Introduction* (London: UCL Press, 1997); Carl Dahlman, 'Diaspora', in *A Companion to Cultural Geography*, ed. by James Duncan and others (Oxford: Blackwell, 2004), pp. 458–98.

new conceptual frameworks required by this ever-increasing human mobility has been a re-examination of ideas of home and 'the relationship between home and homeland, the existence of multiple homes, and the intersections of home, memory, identity and belonging', for example.[4] The opposition between 'home' and 'away' has been challenged and replaced by more open, fluid understandings of what it means to live in different places at different times. Indeed, the very notion of 'place' as static and bounded has been brought into question by conceptualizations that reveal how places are in fact socially constructed, multiply inhabited and constantly reworked by different actors at different times.[5]

However, within transnational research, transnationalism and attachment to place have tended to be seen as incompatible: transnational practices are often conceptualized as being carried out 'across spaces', excluding the possibility of attachments to specific 'places'. More recent attempts to situate, or 'emplace', transnationalism, have been useful in revealing 'the complex interweaving of individuals and social networks within and through places'.[6] However, the focus is predominantly on the macro context, on 'global cities', with little emphasis on the actual place-making practices of migrants within these cities, the specific places they create, or on the situation beyond such contexts.

This article, by contrast, focuses on the micro context: the transnational practices of a migrant group in the small rural town of Gort, in Ireland, a country that until around ten years ago had been characterized by great waves of emigration. It explores how the everyday practices and interactions of the migrants themselves impact upon their situation and the places to which they are connected. Moreover, drawing on conceptualizations of transnationalism and integration, it explores the complex relationship between the two and how it is manifested in this particular case, as well as the wider implications. In particular it draws on notions of place, identity-construction and 'transnational spaces' constructed by Brazilian migrants to explore these relationships, and especially how such spaces relate to their local place-based attachments in the town of Gort.

I propose that far from hindering their local attachment and integration, the 'Brazilianization' and creation of certain transnational spaces by Brazilians in Gort enables a positive engagement with both Irish and Brazilian identities and places. However, the paper also points to questions surrounding the sustainability of such a situation, and the potential limitations of this 'integration' for migrants, given recent and ongoing changes in the socio-economic climate.

---

[4] Alison Blunt and Robyn Dowling, *Home* (Oxford: Routledge, 2006), p. 199.
[5] Rachel Silvey and Victoria Lawson, 'Placing the Migrant', *Annals of the Association of American Geographers*, 89, 1 (1999), 121–32; Michael Peter Smith, *Transnational Urbanism: Locating Globalisation* (Oxford: Blackwell, 2001).
[6] David Conradson and Alan Latham, 'Transnational Urbanism: Attending to Everyday Practices and Mobilities', *Journal of Ethnic and Migration Studies*, 31 (2005), 227–333 (p. 228).

Placing Transnationalism

Since its emergence in the early 1990s as a pertinent concept for describing and analysing exchanges 'involving regular and repeated movements across national boundaries, in which individuals maintain continuous contact with events and other individuals in more that one place',[7] transnationalism has been the subject of much debate, as well as some fierce critique.[8] Points of contention have included doubts as to the actual novelty of the phenomenon;[9] the role of the state in transnational spheres;[10] and the usefulness of the distinction between transnationalism 'from above' and 'from below'.[11]

Further critiques revolve around the dehistoricized nature of transnationalism that ignores the precedents and contexts of the phenomena it studies. These critiques has been further extended to the tendency to 'reify' transnational practices, without due appreciation of the complex other factors and actors at work.[12] However, some useful frameworks of relevance here have been developed. The most important of these is, arguably, Hannerz's 'four organizational frames' to explain a large part of the flow of culture in the world.[13] This analytical framework is extremely useful in understanding the interplay between the macro and the micro — the state, market and forms of life — and the importance of individual and collective agency in cultural change.

More recent conceptualizations of 'transnational social spaces' use a similar approach to Hannerz, but more explicitly evoke the spatiality of these processes and connections.[14] Indeed, just as Hannerz links the large-scale to the mundane and everyday, Faist's 'transnational social spaces' incorporate 'transnational small groups, transnational circuits, and transnational communities'.[15] This perspective, focusing on the wider sociopolitical contexts and their interaction with the

---

[7] Alejandro Portes, 'Introduction: The Debates and Significance of Immigrant Transnationalism', *Global Networks: A Journal of Transnational Affairs*, 1, 3 (2001), 181–94 (p. 182).

[8] Luis Guarnizo and Michael Smith, 'The Locations of Transnationalism,' in *Transnationalism from Below*, ed. by Luis Guarnizo and Michael Smith (London: Transaction, 1998), pp. 3–34.

[9] Portes, p. 182.

[10] Arjun Appadurai, 'Sovereignty Without Territoriality: Notes for a Post-national Geography', in *The Geography of Identity*, ed. by Patricia Yaeger (Ann Arbor: University of Michigan Press, 1996), pp. 40–58.

[11] Guarnizo and Smith, p. 3; *Minor Transnationalism*, ed. by Françoise Lionnet and Shu-Mei Shih (Durham, NC: Duke University Press, 2005).

[12] Roger Waldinger and David Fitzgerald, 'Transnationalism in Question', *American Journal of Sociology*, 109, 5 (2004), 1117–95 (pp. 1186–87).

[13] Ulf Hannerz, *Transnational Connections: Culture, People, Places* (London: Routledge, 1996), p. 70.

[14] See Thomas Faist, 'Transnationalization in International Migration: Implications for the Study of Citizenship and Culture,' *Ethnic and Racial Studies* 3, 2 (2000), 189–222; and *The Volume and Dynamics of International Migration and Transnational Social Spaces* (Oxford: Clarendon Press, 2000).

[15] Faist, p. 191.

concrete changes in peoples' everyday lives and places, is employed in this discussion of Brazilian immigrants in Gort. Yet, I seek to move beyond Faist's 'spaces' to examine more particular places and practices and how they relate to the home-making practices and identities of Brazilians in Gort.

Indeed, within the myriad ways in which 'transnationalism' and the multiple issues related to it have been theorized, perhaps the most useful have been related to place or space: the actual locations in which these 'transnational' or 'integrative' practices and processes occur, and those that they connect. A spatial analysis allows us to move beyond the abstract, conceptual realm, and to consider the concrete, everyday changes in people's lives, and thus examine, as Hannerz suggests, 'both what place does to people and what people do to place'.[16] Brah coins the term 'diaspora space' to encompass not only those who have migrated, but also those who have not — in both receptor and home communities — and thus the term 'includes the genealogies of dispersion with those of staying put'.[17] Indeed, Brah's notion is insightful in that it reveals the dynamic, heterogeneous, and often contested nature of the spaces of diaspora. Brah also suggests ways in which the notion of home within these entangled 'genealogies' can be re-thought, making a distinction between the 'desire for a homeland', and what she terms a 'homing desire'. Rather than yearning for a fixed point of origin (or homeland), a 'homing desire' takes into account the '*multi-locationality* within and across territorial, cultural and psychic boundaries' inherent in diaspora space.[18]

Indeed, scholars have also used this more all-encompassing conceptualization of 'diaspora' to the study of transnationalism, arguing that actual physical migration is not a necessary precondition of participation in 'transnational space'. However, as Crang, Jackson and Dwyer argue, '[w]e must not let the often elite ideology of transnationalism blind us to the practical and emotional importance of attachments to and in place'.[19] Indeed, while acknowledging the multi-dimensionality and heterogeneity of transnational spaces and the increasing porosity of (certain) borders and boundaries, Crang et al.'s research emphasizes the extent to which concrete localities still matter.[20]

Smith's notion of 'transnational urbanism' represents a significant move to bringing some grounding to theories of transnationalism, by capturing 'a sense of the *distanciated* yet *situated* possibilities for constituting and reconstituting social relations'.[21] Smith critiques prevailing 'stucturalist' and 'economistic' approaches to globalization and urban theory, suggesting that both pay little attention to

---

[16] Hannerz, p. 28.
[17] Avtar Brah, *Cartographies of Diaspora: Contesting Identities* (London: Routledge, 1996), p. 184.
[18] Brah, p. 197.
[19] *Transnational Spaces*, ed. by Philip Crang, Peter Jackson and Claire Dwyer (London: Routledge, 2003), pp. 2–3.
[20] See also Conradson and Latham; also Patricia Erkhamp, 'Placing Identities: Transnational Practices and Local Attachments of Turkish Immigrants in Germany,' *Journal of Ethnic and Migration Studies*, 31 (2005), 345–64.
[21] Smith, *Transnational Urbanism*, p. 237.

questions of culture and agency and, indeed, to the socially constructed nature of social relations.[22] He thus favours a more agency-oriented, social constructivist perspective, so as to reconceptualize the urban as 'a social space that is a crossroads or meeting ground for the interplay of diverse localizing practices of national, transnational, and even global-scale actors [...]'.[23] Yet while Smith's analysis is important in challenging prevailing approaches to global change that focus on macro-level processes, the emphasis is still on major cities (such as Los Angeles), and indeed is limited to the US context.

Smaller scale parallel studies in Europe remain limited, although Ehrkamp's study of a neighbourhood inhabited by Turkish immigrants in Germany considers precisely those places *created* by migrants, and provides some fascinating insights into the ways in which transnational practices relate to the construction of spaces of belonging among migrants. Her research focuses mainly on the relationship between identity and place, and challenges the notion of a dichotic relationship between the local and the transnational, which, she argues, 'overly simplif[ies] complex processes of identity construction, assimilation and adaptation'.[24] Indeed, she reveals the subtle interactions of transnational engagement and local feelings of belonging that, far from being merely conflicting, are in fact interconnected in complex ways.

The 'home' has also been conceptualized as a space in which the complex, multi-directional and often contradictory manifestations of transnationalism are played out. Thus, for example, various studies within Al-Ali and Khoser's edited volume reveal the ways in which 'home' — in both its real and symbolic conception — is far from static but rather, 'a dynamic process, involving the acts of imagining, creating, unmaking, changing, losing and moving "homes"'.[25] Botticello's discussion of a Nigerian market in south London points to the ways in which the space acts as a kind of 'home' for the local Nigerian (Yoruba) community.[26] It functions as 'a way of keeping in touch with others who might be neighbours in Nigeria, but must be travelled to in order to remain in neighbourly contact in London'.[27] The practices of the Nigerian users of the market thus reflect a kind of homemaking, by which she takes homemaking to mean 'primarily a social practice that takes place within and through the specific manipulations of any space'.[28]

Finally, as well as the specific sites where transnational processes occur, which can reveal processes whereby migrants create their own places of belonging and

---

[22] Smith, p. 50.
[23] Smith, p. 127.
[24] Erkhamp, p. 348.
[25] Khalid Koser and Nadje Al-Ali, *New Approaches to Migration? Transnational Communities and the Transformation of Home* (London: Routledge, 2002), p. 6.
[26] Julie Botticello, 'Lagos in London: Finding the Space of Home', *Home Cultures*, 4, 1 (2007), 7–24.
[27] Botticello, p. 19.
[28] Botticello, p. 9.

local attachment, another crucial way in which 'place counts'[29] is the actual location of these practices within particular nation states. Thus, the policies of both the sending and receiving states can represent, as Silvey and Lawson argue, 'a mechanism for constructing place and for identifying who has access to certain places and under what conditions'.[30] The subsequent discussion will demonstrate that the practices of Brazilians in Gort reveal how place — in both its material and imaginary senses — is still highly relevant in their negotiation of lives and identities, despite the importance of maintaining ties to the homeland.

Research Context and Methods

Until the mid twentieth century, Gort was a bustling market town and a commercial centre for the surrounding agricultural region. By the 1990s, however, the town had become quiet and sparsely populated as the agricultural industry was in decline and people began moving away.[31] As with many examples of migration flows, the influx of immigrants from Brazil to Gort is a consequence of both macro and micro factors. In 1999, following the example of a poultry factory in the town of Roscommon, Sean Duffy Meat Exports Ltd, located on the outskirts of Gort, applied to the Irish government for overseas work permits and hired eleven people from Vila Fabril, just outside the city of Anápolis in the state of Goiás in central Brazil. All had previously worked in a large meat factory there that had recently closed down. Successive waves of migrants settled in Gort, and at its peak the Brazilian community represented nearly half of the town's population of 3000, although recent reports suggest that many migrants have returned to Brazil as a result of declining economic opportunities.[32]

In a discussion of the transnational practices and integration of Brazilians in Gort, the significance of the particular context in which these processes are occurring — Ireland — cannot be overemphasized, since the debates around these issues have been predominately related to countries where there has been a long history of immigration. In the Irish case, however, the nineteenth and most

---

[29] Peter Kivisto, 'Theorizing Transnational Immigration: A Critical Review of Current Efforts,' *Ethnic and Racial Studies*, 24, 4 (2001), 549–77.

[30] Rachel Silvey and Victoria Lawson, 'Placing the Migrant,' *Annals of the Association of American Geographers*, 89, 1 (1999), 121–32 (p. 128).

[31] Claire Healy, 'Carnaval do Galway: The Brazilian Community in Gort, 1999–2006', *Irish Migration Studies in Latin America*, 4, 3 (2006), 150–53.

[32] Neli Pereira,'Crise obriga imigrantes brasileiros a abandonar "sonho irlandês"', online at <http://www.bbc.co.uk/portuguese/reporterbbc/story/2008/12/081218_brasileirosirlanda_np.shtml> [accessed 7 October 2009]. The term 'community' is problematic when applied to something that may be far from united or static. Indeed, 'Brazilian community' is used here to depict a rather heterogeneous, transient and dynamic group of migrants, but one which is highly recognizable in terms of its sociolinguistic and sociocultural presence and coherence. For a conceptual discussion of community, see Kivisto, p. 573; also Cecelia Menjívar, 'Liminal Legality: Salvadoran and Guatemalan Immigrants' Lives in the US', *American Journal of Sociology*, 111, 4 (2006), 999–1037 (pp. 1024–27).

of the twentieth century were characterized by great waves of Irish emigration, predominantly for economic reasons.[33]

Ireland's economic boom of the 1990s led to huge waves of immigration: net annual inward migration to Ireland increased from 8000 in 1996, to 41,000 in 2002, and remained high at 32,000 in 2004.[34] Many non-EU nationals living in Ireland came, having been offered work permits by Irish employers which, until recently, were almost entirely employer-led and allocated quite unrestrictively. However, the Employment Permits Act, introduced in 2003, gave priority to workers from new EU member states, while imposing a more restrictive skills-based system and requiring an interventionist role for the government.[35] Many of the migrants in Gort were affected by this policy change, and became 'undocumented' either unintentionally, as their existing work permits expired, or knowingly, having entered the country legally but stayed on after their visas expired. They were then living in constant fear of potential deportation.[36]

While the experiences of the Brazilian interviewees varied considerably, all cited economic reasons for coming to Gort. The unstable economic conditions in Brazil since the 1980s, including hyperinflation until 1994, led to low wages and high unemployment.[37] Another 'pull' factor drawing more people to Gort is undoubtedly the existence of strong social networks and what Massey terms the 'cumulative causation' of migration flows.[38] The strong Brazilian presence in Gort thus reduces the costs — both financial and emotional — of migration and this may influence the decision of potential future immigrants. Gort has become a 'first stop' for many new Brazilian migrants to Ireland, who arrive there to find information about issues such as employment and accommodation before moving on to other parts of the country.[39]

---

[33] Many Irish pointed out the striking parallels between the experiences of Brazilians in Ireland, and those of their own Irish relatives in London and the US.

[34] Martin Ruhs, *Managing the Immigration and Employment of Non-EU Nationals in Ireland* (Dublin: The Policy Institute, Trinity College Dublin, 2005), p. 10.

[35] Ruhs, p. xii.

[36] Bill Jordan and Franck Düvell, *Irregular Migration: The Dilemmas of Transnational Mobility* (Cheltenham: Edward Elgar Press, 2002).

[37] Maxine Margolis, *An Invisible Minority: Brazilians in New York City* (Boston, MA: Allyn and Bacon, 1998), p. 11.

[38] Douglas Massey, 'Social Structure, Household Strategies, and the Cumulative Causation of Migration', *Population Index*, 56, 1 (1990), 3–26; see also Franklin Goza, 'Immigrant Social Networks: The Brazilian Case', Working Paper Series 2004-02 (Bowling Green, OH: Center for Family and Demographic Research, Bowling Green State University, 2006), online at <http://www.bgsu.edu/downloads/cas/file35391.pdf> [accessed 7 October 2009].

[39] Brian McGrath, '"*They had already prepared the way*"... Social Capital Formations and Combinations in the Lives of Brazilian Migrants to Ireland' (paper presented to Sociological Association of Ireland Conference 2008, National University of Ireland Galway, 9–11 May 2008), p. 3. For an overview of social capital and migration, see V. Evergeti and E. Zontini, 'Introduction: Some Critical Reflections on Social Capital, Migration and Transnational Families', *Ethnic and Racial Studies*, 29, 6 (2006), 1025–39; Goza, 'Immigrant Social Networks'; and Beatriz Padilla, 'Brazilian Migration to Portugal: Social Networks and Ethnic Solidarity'

The ethnographic research for this study was conducted in Gort, in June 2008. As the principal researcher, I lived with a Brazilian family and thus became an active observer of and participant in informal conversations and everyday activities. Given the small size of the town and the relatively large number of Brazilians, access to their networks was fairly straightforward: participants were found by attending communal meetings such as the Catholic Mass, the Brazilian Women's Group, and the Brazilian 'Quadrilha' Festival, and by social networking using the snowballing technique, since participants would often introduce other potential respondents.[40] The latter technique was facilitated by the strong levels of 'social capital' that exist within the Brazilian community in Gort, whereby people are used to passing on each other's contact details or helping each other with information.

A questionnaire survey (in Portuguese), conducted with twenty-one women and twenty-four men, was used to elicit basic socio-economic data, and twenty-two in depth, semi-structured interviews with Brazilian and Irish residents were carried out. The Brazilian interviewees were selected on the basis of their response to the final survey question, regarding willingness to partake in a longer, more in-depth interview. A representative sample of fifteen was then selected, which aimed to capture as far as possible the diversity of the Brazilian population in Gort with respect to gender, class, regional origin, age and religious affiliation. Irish respondents included the local police Superintendent, the police Ethnic Liaison Officer, a doctor, a community worker, two teachers, a shopkeeper, and a priest. Citation translations are the author's own and all respondents have been anonymized.

Transnational Practices and Places of Belonging: The Brazilian 'Community'

The portrait of Brazilians in Gort presented in this study is based on the experiences conveyed by a small sample on immigrants and local residents, and is thus not intended to be all-inclusive. However, even within this very particular migration flow, there is a great deal of diversity, with regard to factors such as generation, gender, occupation, immigration status, religion and social class. Moreover, while the majority of Brazilians are from the state of Goiás — and the town of Anápolis that the first migrants came from — people from the states of São Paulo, Minas Gerais, Tocantins, and Paraná were also interviewed. In some cases this different migration history was the cause of internal divisions within the community. One of the interviewees, a woman from São Paulo, remarked:

> Até hoje existe como a maioria de aqui é de Anápolis. Eles são um grupo. Não somos muito incluídos — dá para perceber isso. Tem outras pessoas de

(2006), CIES e-working paper 12, online at <http://www.cies.iscte.pt/documents/CIES-WP12.pdf> [accessed 7 October 2009] for a discussion of social capital among Brazilian migrants.
[40] Margolis, p. xi.

São Paulo que pensam, e sentam a mesma coisa que eu. Além de que, dentro de nosso próprio país existe culturas diferentes — então a cultura de lá é diferente.[41]

[Even today the majority [of Brazilians] here are from Anápolis. They are a group, and we're not very much included — they make that clear. There are other people from São Paulo who think and feel the same as I do. Apart from that, even in our own country there are different cultures — so the culture there [in Anápolis] is different.]

She added that she had felt quite excluded when she first arrived in Gort, and had had difficulties finding accommodation, as it seemed that people from Anápolis only helped each other. She described how she had been told of a Brazilian woman who had spare rooms in her house for Brazilians, but that she was met with a very cold response: 'sabia que ela não tinha confiança. Sou Paulista e ela era de Goiás' ['I knew it was because she didn't trust me. I'm a Paulista and she was from Goiás'].[42]

Yet the fundamental experience of having undergone the journey from Brazil and the process of adaptation to an entirely new environment is shared by all, and it is clear that this provides some sense of affinity among them that transcends other markers of difference. When asked if they felt proud to be Brazilian, all respondents replied they were, and that this feeling had been heightened by their migration experience:

Orgulho? Sinto! Quando Brasil ganhou a copa! Estou brincando. Eu amo meu país [...] infelizmente a gente precisa sair, porque tudo mundo busca melhor. Eu sei que aqui é melhor para os meus filhos, mas eu amo meu país — com paixão [...] e agora amo muito mais, estar fora [...] cada coisa — penso na mia Brasil — o que está passando no meu Brasil.[43]

[Proud? Yes, I feel very proud! When Brazil won the World Cup! I am joking. I love my country [...] unfortunately people need to leave, because everyone is looking for a better life. I know that it's better here for my children, but I love my country, passionately! [...]. And now I love it much more, being far away [...] everything — I think of my Brazil — what's happening in my Brazil.]

This remark is reminiscent of Tsuda's discussion of Japanese Brazilian return migrants to Japan whose shared sense of 'Brazilian' identity emerged when faced with negative attitudes towards them in Japan.[44] Yet, as I argue below, this common identity and shared experience of being a Brazilian in Gort by no means represents an alternative to interaction with the local context and people. A discussion of the everyday practices of Gort Brazilians and the places they

---

[41] Amalia, 22 June 2008.
[42] ibid.
[43] Teresa.
[44] Takeyuki Tsuda, 'Transnational Migration and the Nationalisation of Ethnic Identity among Japanese Brazilian Return Migrants,' *Ethos*, 27, 2 (1999), 145–79 (p. 151).

frequent reveals some of the ways in which they negotiate multiple connections, affiliations and belongings.

Spaces of Consumption

There are numerous examples of new places in Gort that have emerged — established by Brazilian migrants themselves — to accommodate the consumption patterns and preferences of the sizeable Brazilian community. With the exception of the internet cafés, which are often used by Irish people, these are predominantly Brazilian places, run by Brazilians and frequented by Brazilians. They include two food shops selling Brazilian produce, two fashion shops, four beauty salons, three internet cafés and two money transfer places, as well as private cooks, babysitters, and taxi services within the community.

Food is an important aspect of the everyday lives of Gort Brazilians, and the availability of Brazilian food is central to their feeling of being at home. Gort has two shops selling food products imported from Brazil, including meat, rice, maize, manioc, beans, herbs and spices, as well as cakes and confectionery. Although the majority of respondents say they shop mainly in supermarkets, because they are much cheaper, all claim they use the Brazilian shops to get hold of certain products unavailable elsewhere. Many also commented on the fact that beans and rice — staples in the Brazilian diet — are now available in Gort's supermarkets. Ana commented:

> É melhor porque pode comprar tudo aqui. Quando eu cheguei não tinha arroz — as crianças queriam mas não tinha porque só tinha na fruteira. Acabava — havia pouco.[45]
>
> [It's better [now] because we can buy everything here. When I arrived you couldn't buy rice — my children wanted it, but there wasn't any because they only had it in the greengrocer's. It used to run out — there wasn't much.]

Brazilian dishes are also prepared and sold by community members such as Dona Rita, who runs a very successful business preparing large vats of beans, rice, meat and salad; people who have little time to cook between working shifts have this food delivered, or buy it as a take-away, or eat it at her house. I went to interview her at her home one day at lunchtime and within the two hours that I was there eight people dropped in to collect ready-prepared portions of food for themselves and their friends or families. Dona Rita has been living in Gort for nearly five years, along with her youngest son and daughter-in-law, in a house on one of the new housing estates. Since she is undocumented, and speaks very little English, cooking for fellow Brazilians is a viable way to earn an income using her skills. It has also enabled her to make contacts throughout the Brazilian community, and also with Irish people in the wider community:

---

[45] Interview carried out 17 June 2008.

> Tenho muitos amigos brasileiros e eles falam de mim para os amigos irlandeses deles... e agora são amigos meus. Os irlandeses são muito bons [...] e gostam de ter amigos brasileiros.[46]
>
> [I am friends with lots of Brazilians and they tell Irish people about me and now they are my friends. The Irish are very nice people [...] and they like to make friends with Brazilians.]

In addition to food, personal appearance is clearly an important part of the lives of Brazilians in Gort, demonstrated by the presence of four specifically Brazilian beauty salons that have emerged, offering various hair and beauty treatments at far lower prices than their Irish equivalents in the town. As well as reflecting the importance of appearance for Brazilian women (three respondents have their nails painted and hair styled every week), they are important places for social interaction. Amalia, for example, states that she sees very few people in her day-to-day life as a cleaner for two Irish households who are out at work when she cleans, and her husband works long hours, so her trips to the beauty salon are social occasions, where she can catch up with local gossip by chatting with other Brazilian women (interview, 21 June 2008). Indeed, she had found one of her cleaning jobs through a woman at the salon. Echoing the practices of Brazilian migrants in Lisbon discussed by Padilla, the beauty salons thus represent a means of access to social networks for some Brazilian women in Gort. Padilla points to the gendered dimensions of such networks suggesting that, due to the nature or their work, women often have less access to resources than men.[47] My interviews with women in Gort revealed similar patterns. However, those who had been there for longer were more active in the social networks, often more so than men, suggesting that their access to resources was cumulative, and improved over time.

The shop 'Brazilian Fashions and Parties of Brazil', which specializes in clothes and shoes imported from Brazil, was opened in November 2007 in response to high demand since, as recounted by João who has lived in Gort for five years: 'Os sapatos aqui não são como os sapatos no Brasil. A forma... tudo é diferente. É legal que agora a gente pode comprar sapatos brasileiros aqui' [the shoes here aren't the same as in Brazil. The design is different. It's great that we can get Brazilian shoes here now].[48] When asked in what ways she felt proud to be Brazilian, Maria, one of the first Brazilians to come to Gort, in 1999, said: 'Eu gosto do estilo de roupa das mulheres brasileiras. Aqui a gente tem que levar mais roupa, mas fazemos muito esforço para vestir elegantemente' [I like the way that Brazilian women dress. We have to cover up more here [because of the cold], but we make a lot of effort to dress up nicely].[49] Such remarks suggest that fashion

---

[46] Dona Rita, 18 June 2008.
[47] Padilla, p. 10; see also Ana Cristina Martes Braga, *Brasileiros nos Estados Unidos: um estudo sobre imigrantes em Massachusetts* (São Paulo: Paz e Terra, 2000).
[48] 13 June 2008.
[49] 16 June 2008.

and appearance thus represent important elements in maintaining — or creating — a sense of Brazilian identity in Gort.

Religious Practices

'O brasileiro é um povo de fé — tem muita fé' [Brazilians are a people with faith — they have a lot of faith].[50] Such a remark is evidenced in the multiple religious groups that exist within Gort. Of the forty-five Brazilians who responded to the questionnaire, thirty-eight said that they were a member of a church, and attend congregations in Gort. As well as a weekly Catholic Mass in Portuguese (given by an Irish priest, a missionary in Brazil for many years), there are six different Evangelical (Pentecostal) Churches, established by Brazilians (indeed, one was established while I was there), which represent important places of social support and interaction, as well as spiritual engagement.[51] These range from the internationally established 'Assembleia de Deus' [Assembly of God], the premises of which are in a smart modern building near the centre, to much smaller sects, including one established above a pub.

The Churches clearly represent key sites for enabling migrants to maintain direct links with Brazil. This included inviting priests or pastors from their home communities, or celebrating traditional Brazilian religious festivals in parallel to their friends and relatives back home.[52] Services are conducted in Portuguese and attended almost entirely by Brazilians. When asked whether he felt that celebrating Mass in Portuguese further discouraged people from learning English, and whether he felt it would be better for them to attend the Mass in English, the Catholic priest replied:

> [...] it's not just a question that our Mass is in Portuguese, but it's the way it's celebrated that is different. It's got a lot to do with time — people feel that here the Mass is just 'you go in, then you get out after twenty minutes', they don't feel they've been to Mass.[53]

[50] Roberto, 11 June 2008.
[51] Regarding the supportive role of the churches among Brazilian migrants in Florida, see José Cláudio Souza Alves and Lúcia Ribeiro, 'Migracão, Religião e Transnacionalismo: o caso dos brasileiros no sul da Flórida', *Religião e Sociedade*, 22, 2 (2002), 65–90. Regarding the importance of religion among migrants see Jacqueline Hagan and Helen Ebaugh, 'Calling Upon the Sacred: Migrants' Use of Religion in the Migration Process', *International Migration Review*, 37, 4 (2006), 1145–62; Adriana Kemp and Rebecca Raijman, 'Christian Zionists in the Holy Land: Evangelical Churches, Labor Migrants, and the Jewish State', *Identities: Global Studies in Power and Culture*, 10, 3 (2003), 295–318; Manuel Vasquez and Marie Friedman Marquardt, *Globalising the Sacred: Religion Across the Americas* (New Jersey: Rutgers University Press, 2003); and Menjivar, 'Liminal Legality'.
[52] See Peggy Levitt, *God Needs No Passport: Immigrants and the Changing American Religious Landscape* (New York: New York Press, 2007) for a discussion of how religious 'institutions' create and enable transnational religious networks; Cecilia Menjivar, 'Religious Institutions and Transnationalism: A Case Study of Catholic and Evangelical Salvadoran Immigrants', *International Journal of Politics, Culture & Society*, 12, 4 (1999), 589–612; and Helen R. Ebaugh and Janet S. Chafetz, *Religion and the New Immigrants* (Walnut Creek, CA: AltaMira Press, 2000).
[53] 6 June 2008. Interview conducted in English.

He also said that an important part of the service is the social gathering afterwards over coffee, where people can chat to each other and make connections. The Catholic Church also organizes different activities including English classes, catechism, and a women's group. Evidently both Catholic and Pentecostal Churches function as a source of social support and interaction for Gort Brazilians, in addition to playing an important spiritual role. The Pastor of the evangelical 'Assembleia de Deus' commented:

> Our principal role is to provide spiritual support. We want to encourage people to have optimism [...] but we also organize many social activities, such as camps for young people, dance classes, theatre workshops, and English classes. We also keep people up to date with legislative changes that affect the Brazilian community.[54]

Some respondents claim to have changed their church-going practices since living in Gort, moving either to a different branch of Pentecostalism, or from the Catholic to a Pentecostal church. Tereza, who works full time as a chef in a local restaurant, goes to services at different evangelical churches depending on her shifts, but rarely goes to the Catholic Mass (which is at five o'clock on a Sunday) as she is nearly always working. Thus, while she holds a strong personal belief in God and prays a lot, her choice of church is more a practical, as opposed to a spiritual, choice:

> Olha aqui tem diversas igrejas [...] aqui tem mistura de católico com evangélico com deus de amor, Universal. Eu quando comecei, sempre tem grupo de brasileiros — para fazer amizades, conhecer a pessoas — sabe — você escolhe uma igreja [...] eu fui à Universal[55] — é muito boa [...] gostei, eu freqüentei'.[56]
>
> [Well, there are various churches here [...] here we've got a mix of Catholic, with evangelical, with charismatic, the Universal. When I got here, I wanted to meet other Brazilians — to make friends, get to know people, you know, you choose a church [...] I went to the Universal, it's very good [...] I liked it, so I went [to services] there.]

So while religious practices reflect the importance of faith among Gort Brazilians, church-going and participation in church-related activities can also represent an individual strategy for coping with the challenges of adapting to such a different setting and for keeping in touch with 'home'. While these religious practices may reflect important ways in which Gort Brazilians engage within a 'transnational social space', creating 'alternative allegiances' to those that exist in Gort, they also play, in many cases, a key role in their process of adaptation

---

[54] 10 June 2008. Interview conducted in English.
[55] *Igreja Universal do Reino de Deus* [Universal Church of the Kingdom of God] — another well-established international faction of the Pentecostal church.
[56] 9 June 2008.

to life in the town.[57] This echoes elements of Levitt's discussion of the multiple dimensions of religion and transnational migration in which she describes how religious activities can in fact promote integration, through providing immigrants with a sense of belonging.[58] Moreover, these practices take place within, and are very much associated with, specific locations and contexts in Gort. As Vasquez and Marquardt argue in their discussion of Latino immigrant churches in Atlanta, these places, far from being 'deterritorialized' are shaped by 'global economic change, transnational migration *and* local historical factors.'[59]

Keeping in Touch with Brazil

Many theorists of transnationalism have pointed to how technological advances have expanded the scope, and increased the rate, of transnational connections.[60] As Margolis writes in her discussion of Brazilian immigrants in New York City, 'the dual orientation of Brazilians and other transnational migrants is partly dependent on modern communication and transport networks'.[61] Modern technology is undoubtedly fundamental to the transnational lives of Brazilian migrants in Gort. Most households have bought a digibox or satellite dish and regularly watch Brazilian television, including soap operas, news and sport. Indeed, watching the latest *telenovela* (soap opera) seemed to be a regular evening activity. Moreover, all the Brazilians regularly call friends and relatives in Brazil, taking advantage of the widely available mobile phone deals offering cheap rates. The internet is also commonly used as a means to keep in touch with people and events in Brazil (and elsewhere). One of the interviewees recounted that when they have parties and celebrations at his house, they often share the experience with their family in Brazil via their webcam (Luis, 10 June 2008). However, while such practices are undoubtedly 'transnational', in that they reveal direct ties to Brazil and involvement with people and events there, they do not seem to reflect a sense of 'in-betweeness' — being 'neither here nor there' — as described in Margolis's study, or in Cwerner's discussion of Brazilians in London.[62] Indeed, while the majority of respondents claim to send money back to Brazil — predominantly for personal investments — and indeed worked extremely long hours to do so, this did not seem to imply sacrificing the creation of a 'home' in Gort. Rather than putting their lives on hold, my interviewees were, on the

---

[57] Peggy Levitt, '"You Know, Abraham Was Really the First Immigrant": Religion and Transnational Migration,' *International Migration Review*, 37, 3 (2003), 847–73 (p. 851).
[58] Levitt, *God Needs No Passport*, p. 886.
[59] Vasquez and Marquardt, p. 146; my emphasis.
[60] See Faist, 'Transnationalization', and Steven Vertovec, 'Cheap Calls: The Social Glue of Migrant Transnationalism', *Global Networks: Journal of Transnational Affairs*, 4, 2 (2000), 219–24.
[61] Margolis, p. 114.
[62] Margolis; Saulo Cwerner, 'The Times of Migration', *Journal of Ethnic and Migration Studies*, 27, 2 (2001), 7–36.

whole, keen to live and make the most of their lives in Gort at the same time as preparing for the future:

> Mas há que viver aqui também. [...]. Primeiro eu faço as minhas necessidades, e todo o que sobra é para Brasil. Porque eu estou vivendo aqui, preciso de dinheiro aqui.[63]
>
> [You have to live here too. [...]. First I meet my own needs, and then everything that's left I send back to Brazil. Because I'm living here now, I need money here.]

Everyday Lives and Social Capital

Despite its inherent diversity, there is an established Brazilian 'community' in Gort, with a visible presence and a web of complex social networks functioning at all levels of the migration process.[64] For many, the strong Brazilian presence exerts a very positive aspect on their lives. Luis, who has lived in Gort for six years, states:

> A gente tem chopes brasileiros, a gente tem bancos brasileiros para transferir dinheiro, você tem amigos, você tem parentes, você conhece outras pessoas, você tem festa [...] é ótimo. Eu não mudaria de Gort a não ser por motivo muito forte. Gort é um pedaço de Brasil. Quando cheguei aqui, eram cinqüenta brasileiros, agora tem dois mil.[65]
>
> [We have Brazilian shops, we have Brazilian banks to send money, we have friends, we have relatives, we know lots of people, we have parties — it's great. I wouldn't leave Gort unless it was for a very good reason. Gort is part of Brazil. When I arrived here there were fifty Brazilians, now there are two thousand.]

While his estimate of the number of Brazilians in Gort is a little exaggerated, it demonstrates how the number of Brazilians and the integration among them makes his life in Gort a happy one. Others also described how having other Brazilians around has helped them enormously. Beatriz, who works occasionally as a cleaner or babysitter for other Brazilians adds:

> Sim, porque realmente para conseguir trabalho aqui tem que ser por amizade. [...]. Sempre é assim, os irlandeses sempre procuram um brasileiro para procurar outro brasileiro. É assim que a gente consegue trabalho.[66]
>
> [Yes, because in order find work here it has to be through a friend [...]. It's always like that. Irish people always look for a Brazilian person to find another Brazilian [...]. That's how we find jobs.]

For many, the presence of other Brazilians was the main reason they came to Gort in the first place. Amalia, who arrived in 2003 but had to wait a year before

---
[63] João, 13 June 2008.
[64] McGrath, esp. p. 3.
[65] 10 June 2008.
[66] 17 June 2008.

finally being able to bring her daughter over, states:

> Eu achei que ficando em Gort, porque tem tantos brasileiros, ela ia ter também amigas brasileiras. E isso ajudaria na adaptação dela [...]. E por um lado é boa aqui por ter muitos brasileiros porque aqui eu consigo pessoas para mim para cuidar dela para mim trabalhar.[67]
>
> [I thought that being in Gort, because there were so many Brazilians here, she would have Brazilian friends too, and that would help her to settle in [...]. In a way it's good having lots of Brazilians here, because I can find people to look after my daughter for me so I can go to work.]

Many Brazilians who have been in Gort for a long time believe that the situation for recent arrivals is much easier as 'there's always someone who can help them. There are lots of people who speak English now who can help them'.[68]

Over the last four years at least six new housing estates have been built to house Gort's rapidly increasing population, and, because of the long waiting lists to get houses on the new estates, many households comprise two or more Brazilian families or extended families. Maria adds:

> When I first came it was really hard. There was nowhere to live. Eight of us had to share one room in a horrible flat. Now there are lots of houses, but they weren't here before.[69]

Some respondents did point to the negative aspects of having so many Brazilians in Gort. Sandra, who has lived there for seven years, said that things are worse now and some individuals give the community a bad name:

> Sempre há histórias ruins sobre os brasileiros em Gort. Pessoas que dirigem bêbados, motoristas maus [...]. Problemas demais com os brasileiros em Gort.[70]
>
> [You're always hearing bad things about the Brazilians in Gort. About people who drive when they're drunk, bad drivers [...]. Too many problems with the Brazilians in Gort.]

Other people said that there is now much more competition for jobs, particularly for women in the cleaning sector, so people are forced to look elsewhere for work. Moreover, cases of people being exploited by other Brazilians, including being sold jobs or given false information, were also recounted.

A key factor in the unequal power dynamics within the community is the varying levels of language ability, or, what Bourdieu terms 'linguistic capital': the mastery of a language as a form of cultural capital that implies a higher social status.[71] Indeed, language acquisition is undoubtedly a major factor contributing

---

[67] 21 June 2008.
[68] Carlos, 16 June 2008.
[69] 16 June 2008.
[70] 9 June 2008.
[71] Pierre Bourdieu, *Reproduction in Education, Society and Culture* (London: Sage Publications, 1990), p. 114.

to the experience of Brazilians in Gort and speaking English is clearly seen as an important form of social capital, or linguistic capital — a means of being more flexible, having more opportunities and of avoiding being exploited. However, many mentioned that the very fact there are so many Brazilians means they are less likely to learn English. Beatriz remarks:

> A gente acomoda demais [...] por que eu vou no mercado, tem brasileiros que me atendem, na farmácia [...] não tem lugar onde a gente não me atende em português, então a gente se acomoda, e na rua a gente encontra amigos brasileiros.[72]
>
> [We feel too much at home [...] because when I go into the shop it's always Brazilians who serve me, and in the chemist's [...] there's nowhere here where they don't serve me in Portuguese, so people get used to it, and in the street we bump into Brazilian friends.]

On the other hand, while the presence of such a significant Brazilian community in Gort means that people always have someone to talk to in Portuguese, the increased competition for jobs, and a growing awareness of the advantages of linguistic capital, appear to be creating a greater incentive to learn English. This is confirmed by the many English classes available in the town, including those offered by the churches, by private tutors and at a private language school. In addition, a government-funded ESOL programme was set up in Gort in September 2006, and appears to be attended by both men and women. While McGrath argues that the lack of linguistic capital represents a barrier to wider integration among Gort Brazilians,[73] I would suggest that the more widespread recognition of the advantages of this 'linguistic capital' is in fact a factor in the gradual process of social integration into life in Gort. The increasing numbers of language classes on offer are in response to high demand, and a widespread recognition within the community of how a knowledge of English is essential for overcoming some of the unequal power dynamics within the community.

My research visit to Gort coincided with the 'Quadrilha' carnival, a traditional Brazilian (originally Portuguese) festival to celebrate the *dia de São João*, which has taken place annually in Gort's main square since 2003. The event was organized by volunteers within the Brazilian community, including Maria, who choreographed many of the traditional dances and helped put together the extravagant, brightly coloured costumes and outfits. For one day, Gort's main square takes on an entirely different identity, becoming re-imagined and re-fashioned. The festival went ahead despite heavy rain, and some Irish joined in the dancing and sampled the Brazilian food and drink. Some parallels may be drawn with Law's discussion of Filipino domestic workers in Hong Kong who gather in a central square every Sunday.[74] While the Quadrilha carnival is an annual event, it perhaps reflects,

---

[72] 17 June 2008.
[73] McGrath, p. 7.
[74] Lisa Law, 'Home Cooking: Filipino Women and Geographies of the Senses in Hong Kong', *Ecumene*, 8, 3 (2001), 264–83.

as in the case of the Hong Kong Filipinas, 'a conscious invention of home, and imagining of place through food and other sensory practices'.[75] Yet this evocation or 'invention' of home by Gort Brazilians is not an escape from the local reality, but rather an active and positive engagement with it, a means of creating a sense of belonging in the town.

Conclusions

There are distinctly Brazilian places in Gort, fundamental to the everyday lives of its Brazilian, 'transnational', community. Such localities enable them to maintain ties with people, places and events in Brazil, as well as to adopt a Brazilian identification strategy in Gort, and they also represent important sites of social interaction and support among members of the community. However, while all these places may form part of what Faist describes as a 'transnational community' in a 'transnational social space', there is also a strong sense of attachment to Gort and an awareness of the local context. For many, it is the sense of belonging and security that they feel through the existence of these places that makes them feel more at home there.

In a discussion of some of the places frequented or used by Gort Brazilians, such as shops, churches and beauty salons, this paper reveals how, rather than occupying an abstract space that transcends both 'here' and 'there', place plays a crucial role in their experiences of migration, adaptation and 'local meaning making'.[76] Transnational ties and local attachment can be 'complementary' and such dual attachments in fact represent ways in which migrants negotiate 'different scales of belonging'.[77] It was beyond the scope of the study to examine in depth the varying combinations of 'transnationalism' and 'integration' manifested in the experiences of Brazilians in Gort.[78] However, this research illustrates how the everyday practices of migrants can reveal the fluid and multifaceted nature of identity and belonging, and how places themselves are dynamic and transient, and can also be important agents of change through the process of being transformed and re-fashioned.

While this study corroborates the notion that transnational practices, and the creation of Brazilian spaces within Gort, do not encumber the feelings of local attachment among Brazilian migrants, academics and researchers need to look at the wider context and the considerable structural barriers to immigrant integration. Indeed, while faith communities have been recognized as being important

---

[75] Law, p. 276.
[76] Guarnizo and Smith, p. 12.
[77] Erkhamp, p. 361.
[78] Ewa Morawska, 'Immigrant Transnationalism and Assimilation: A Variety of Combinations and the Analytic Strategy it Suggests', in *Toward Assimilation and Citizenship: Immigrants in Liberal Nation-States*, ed. by Christian Joppke and Ewa Morawska (New York: Palgrave Macmillan, 2003), pp. 133–76.

arenas for the formulation of social capital, Alba and Foner remind us that we must also 'bear in mind that there are profound inequalities that create nonreligious barriers to inclusion'.[79] The current downturn in the Irish economy, and the increasing numbers of migrants in Gort who are 'undocumented', suggest fundamental challenges to the current — predominantly positive — situation.

Transnational practices can in fact *enable* a sense of local attachment and, rather than challenging the integrity of the nation state, they form part of the process of its inevitable renegotiation and transformation. Micro studies such as this reveal how integration cannot be dictated or enforced by top-down measures involving rigid lists of rules, restrictions and sanctions. Rather, such policies need to engage with the actual practices of migrants themselves and acknowledge their different 'scales of belonging'.[80] While the situation in Gort is a small case study in a particular context, it very effectively illuminates potential areas for research within a wider framework. It is only through an understanding of certain 'minor' practices of transnationality and of how migrants adapt to particular places, that 'major' policies related to migrants — before, during, and after they have migrated — can be truly relevant to, and reflective of, the realities they live and experience.

This research was funded by the Economic and Social Research Council. I would also like to thank Frank Murray for his help and support during my visit to Gort; Dr Cathy McIlwaine and Dr Jaine Beswick for their extremely useful comments on the drafts of the paper; and in particular, the Brazilian and Irish families and individuals who gave up their time to participate in this study.

QUEEN MARY, UNIVERSITY OF LONDON

---

[79] Richard Alba and Nancy Foner, 'Immigrant Religion in the US and Western Europe: Bridge or Barrier to Inclusion?', *International Migration Review*, 42, 2 (2008), 360–92 (p. 384).
[80] Erkhamp, p. 361.

Migrant Languages in a Multi-Ethnic Scenario: Brazilian Portuguese-Speakers in London

ANA SOUZA

Introduction

The focus of this paper is the use of the Portuguese language in identification practices by a small group of Brazilians living in the Brazilian community of London.[1] I firstly aim to provide a general account of the main political, social, demographic, cultural and linguistic factors affecting these Brazilian migrants, examining in particular the links between language and identity from the perspective of a group of mothers who take their children to Portuguese lessons. I then focus on three of the offspring to assess how they are affected by their mothers' self-identification. Hence, this paper seeks to provide insight on the importance of language in the construction of identity of a group of mothers of Brazilian heritage in England, and how their positioning affects their children's identification and linguistic practices.

Theoretical Background

The relationship between language and ethnic identity (defined here as an individual level of identification with a cultural group)[2] is a recurrent topic in academic treatises, but the evaluation of its importance in different contexts varies between scholars. Khemlani-David, for example, highlights the apparent lack of any correlation between language use and identity marking by the Sindhis in Malaysia, who appear to be shifting to the English language but who continue to maintain their ethnic customs, culture, and religion.[3] On the other

---

[1] Group diversity regarding reasons for immigration, the time of arrival, the type of lifestyle and perceived status in the new country, can render the labelling of such a group as a single community with uniform characteristics rather difficult; see, for example, Maxine Margolis, *Little Brazil: An Ethnography of Brazilian Immigrants in New York City* (Princeton, NJ: Princeton University Press, 1994), pp. 18–19. However, I adopt the definition of community as elaborated by Anderson and delineated in this issue by Beswick and Pozo-Gutiérrez, see Benedict Anderson, *Imagined Communities: Reflection on the Origins and Spread of Nationalism*, rev. edn (London and New York: Verso, 1991), and also Paul Taylor, John Richardson, Alan Yeo and Ian Marsh, *Sociology in Focus* (Ormskirk, Lancs: Causeway Press, 1995), p. 387.

[2] John Hutchinson and Anthony Smith, 'Introduction', in *Ethnicity*, ed. by John Hutchinson and Anthony Smith (Oxford: Oxford University Press, 1996), pp. 3–14 (p. 5).

[3] Maya Khemlani-David, 'Language Shift, Cultural Maintenance, and Ethnic Identity: A Study of a Minority Community. The Sindhis of Malaysia', *International Journal of Sociology of Language*, 130 (1998), 67–76 (pp. 75–76).

hand, Liebkind believes that 'language can become the most important symbol of ethnic identity',[4] and that the association between language and identity is dependent on the social context of particular groups.

In order to explore the perspectives of Brazilian women and of their children regarding the relationship between language and identity in a migrant context, this study draws on Tajfel, who has designed 'one of the most notable theories of social identity'.[5] Tajfel categorizes migrants into three types: those who wish to assimilate,[6] and thus assume many characteristics (language, culture, social norms, among others) of the receptor society; those who totally oppose assimilation and thus retain most of the characteristics of their autochthonous group; and those who adopt certain characteristics of the receptor society but retain others from their own group.[7] Using this categorization to examine the mothers' collective goals in relation to the receptor society and the types of migrants which represent their sense of identity is a useful starting point for understanding the relationship between language and identity in this case. Indeed, the emotional significance of group identity seems to be the main reason for the use of Portuguese by this group of mothers within the Brazilian community. This emotional importance of group self-concept is used by Tajfel, who describes social identity as:

> that part of an individual's self-concept which derives from their knowledge of their membership in a social group together with the values and emotional significance attached to that membership.[8]

Social identity is also a result of the comparisons individuals make between their groups with other groups. Tajfel argues that the search for a positive image at the centre of the construction of social identity leads individuals to try to interact with the receptor group free of the constraints caused by their diverse ethnic backgrounds.[9] In other words, individuals try to integrate in different degrees into the receptor society. Bauman, however, argues that assimilation can never be fully successful because the process of gaining cultural

---

[4] Karmela Liebkind, 'Social Psychology', in *Handbook of Language and Ethnic Identity*, ed. by Joshua A. Fishman (Oxford: Oxford University Press, 1999), pp. 140–51 (p. 143).

[5] Jette Hansen and Jun Liu, 'Social Identity and Language: Theoretical and Methodological Issues', *TESOL Quarterly*, 31, 3 (1997), 567–76 (p. 567).

[6] The wish to assimilate could reflect a need imposed on migrants by the receptor society, as discussed by Ien Ang, *On Not Speaking Chinese: Living Between Asia and the West* (London: Routledge, 2001), pp. 27 and 65. I use the term 'assimilation' here as it is employed in the original work of the authors mentioned in the text, but I am aware that it fails to reflect the migrant's willingness (agency) to participate in the receptor society. Focusing on the relationship between language and identity, this willingness relates to learning a language in order to become a member of the group that speaks it (Bernard Spolsky, 'Second-Language Learning', *Handbook of Language and Ethnic Identity*, ed. by Joshua A. Fishman (Oxford: Oxford University Press, 1999), 181–92 (p. 189)).

[7] Henri Tajfel, *The Social Psychology of Minorities* (London: Minority Rights Group, 1978).

[8] Henri Tajfel, *Human Groups & Social Categories: Studies in Social Psychology* (Cambridge: Cambridge University Press, 1981), p. 255.

[9] Tajfel, *Social Psychology of Minorities*, p. 14.

traits which are inherited by the receptor community does not allow members of the minority group to be exactly like receptor members.[10] In contrast to Bauman, Berry, a social psychologist, not only accepts assimilation as one of the possible ways members of minority groups relate to the receptor group, but adds another scenario, that of marginalization — the relationship between groups where both the cultures are rejected by the members of the minority group.[11] As a result, Berry presents a fourfold theory where intergroup contact can result in integration (keeping some cultural features while participating in the receptor society), assimilation (original cultural features are replaced by the receptor ones), separation (only the minority cultural features are valued), or marginalization (neither the receptor nor the minority features are valued).

In spite of frequently being used in social psychology, fourfold theories as advocated by Berry have been criticized by a number of researchers such as Rudmin. Rudmin's criticisms are based on the fact that 'defining acculturation types by two cultures, two attitudes, two identities, or two languages does not result in four possible types but sixteen'.[12] Using logic, the number of possible types increases to 256 in cases where the types 'are defined by choices of three cultures [...] or defined by choices of two cultures and by whether the choices are freely made versus imposed'.[13]

Another criticism of social psychology is that the theories of acculturation tend to present the types of intergroup relations as fixed. The intergroup approach to second language acquisition (SLA) described by Giles and Byrne,[14] for example, has already been criticized for portraying identity as unitary and fixed,[15] which does not represent the reality of the multilingual individuals experiencing life in times of globalization.[16] Therefore I relate Tajfel's three types of minorities to the types of identification adopted by members of migrant groups as described by Block as: (1) going 'native', (2) becoming (early/expatriate) 'cosmopolitans', and (3) remaining 'tourists'.[17] My contention is that these types of identification are part of a continuum, where migrant group members who reject any direct involvement in the receptor society (the 'tourists') and those who seek and desire

---

[10] Ang, p. 5. See also Zygmunt Bauman, 'The Social Manipulation of Morality: Moralizing Actors, Diaphorizing Action', *Theory, Culture and Society*, 8 (1991), 137–51.

[11] Karmela Liebkind, p. 142.

[12] Floyd Rudmin, 'Critical History of the Acculturation Psychology of Assimilation, Separation, Integration, and Marginalization', *Review of General Psychology*, 7, 1 (2003), 3–37 (p. 3).

[13] Rudmin, p. 25.

[14] Howard Giles and Jane Byrne, 'An Intergroup Approach to Second Language Acquisition', *Journal of Multilingual and Multicultural Development*, 3, 1 (1982), 17–40.

[15] Bonny Norton, *Identity and Language Learning: Gender, Ethnicity and Educational Change* (London: Longman, 2000).

[16] *Negotiation of Identities in Multilingual Contexts*, ed. by Aneta Pavlenko and Adrian Blackledge (Clevedon: Multilingual Matters, 2004), p. 5.

[17] David Block, 'Destabilized Identities and Cosmopolitanism across Language and Cultural Borders: Two Case Studies', *Hong Kong Journal of Applied Linguistics*, 7, 2 (2002), 1–11.

full integration into the receptor society represent the limit cases, while those who are willing to adopt certain characteristics of the receptor group, whilst retaining others from their own ethnic group (the 'cosmopolitans'), take a middle line. The use of such a continuum also recognizes that these identifications are not static and invariable, but can move along between the two extremes. In other words, people's identification may vary according to social context.

The Context: Brazilians in London

The political and economic situation of Brazil in the 1980s forced Brazilian nationals to migrate in search of work opportunities abroad. In her book about the effects of immigration on the change of gender roles in Brazilian families living in the United States, Debiaggi describes this situation in these terms:

> At the individual level it might be said that the push factors for Brazilians to leave the country are linked to economics. In fact, the emigration floodgates opened at the time that the Cruzado Plan, the government's attempt to control inflation, failed in 1986. Brazil at that time was faced with the saying 'it has to work', but it did not. 'The new generation gets desperate with the lack of opportunities in Brazil and searches for alternatives ('O povo da diáspora', 8 July 1991). Moreover, many middle-class professionals in Brazil were either unable to find a job in the field of their training or even if employed, received salaries so low they were forced to hold two or three jobs in order to meet their needs. A middle-class standard of living was, and continues to be, increasingly difficult to sustain. The search for a better future for the next generation constitutes another motivational factor linked to economics. Brazilians no longer see the possibility of providing good quality education for their children in their own country. A good education means having one's children in private schools, which present higher costs each year ('Aumenta êxodo', 11 April 1990). These circumstances continue to apply.[18]

The number of Brazilians in the US in 2000 was estimated to be over 800,000, making it their main migratory destination.[19] However, the severe restrictions on entry to the US that are now imposed have greatly affected the number of Brazilians migrating there. In Europe, the UK has become one of the most significant European destinations for them. According to official estimates there are now about 150,000 Brazilians in the UK;[20] however, informal figures place the number of Brazilians currently living in London alone at anywhere between 30,000 and 200,000.[21] Many of the Brazilians coming to the UK are descended from European

---

[18] Sylvia Debiaggi, *Changing Gender Roles: Brazilian Immigrant Families in the US* (New York: LFB Scholarly, 2002).
[19] *IBGE* (Brazilian Institute for National Statistics) 2004, online at <www.ibge.gov.br/home/estatistica/populacao/censo2000/atlas/pag021.pdf> [accessed 8 October 2009].
[20] See online at <http://sistemas.mre.gov.br/kitweb/datafiles/BRMundo/pt-br/file/Brasileiros no Mundo-Estimativas.pdf> [accessed 8 October 2009].
[21] Saulo Cwerner, 'Times of Migration', *Journal of Ethnic and Migration Studies*, 27, 1 (2001), 7–36; Yara Evans, Jane Wills, Kavita Datta, Joanna Herbert, Cathy McIlwaine, Jon May, Father

families who migrated to Brazil in the nineteenth and twentieth centuries, primarily for socio-economic and political reasons, such as taking up work after the abolition of slavery in Brazil, or to escape the two world wars.[22] As a consequence, many Brazilians hold European passports and are therefore free to enter the UK.

However, the many Brazilian nationals living in London do not constitute a close-knit group; instead, Brazilians are spread all over the city. This characteristic alone makes the Brazilian group different from other ethnic groups in London which tend to be concentrated in one area, such as Punjabis in Southall, Jamaicans in Harlesden or Bangladeshis in Tower Hamlets. Nevertheless, their cultural impact has been great. In London many services, from tarot reading to legal aid, are offered in Portuguese by Brazilian nationals. It is also possible to attend religious services in Brazilian Portuguese in both Catholic and Protestant churches, and there are also celebrations of other religions which were mainly developed in Brazil, such as Kardecism and Afro-Brazilian cults. The Brazilian government has also exploited international interest in Brazilian culture and has promoted many cultural events in London. These take place throughout the year, but especially during the summer months.[23] They involve artists who come from Brazil specially to perform, as well as groups based in the UK and other countries.

In addition to the cultural presence of Brazil in London, the growing number of Brazilian migrants has also led to the development of organizations, such as ABRAS (Brazilian Association) and ABRIR (Brazilian Association of Educational Projects in the UK).[24] This latter association resulted from the interest shown by Brazilians in maintaining their language through the organization of playgroups by Brazilian mothers, as well as the participation of a group which offers literacy classes in Portuguese. As the description above indicates, it is possible for Brazilians to live in London and use Portuguese for most of the activities in their daily lives. However, the fact that Portuguese is a standardized language and follows the Roman alphabet, only differing from English in having three fewer letters and the use of accents, facilitates the learning of English by Portuguese speakers and vice versa.

However, in the study on which this paper is based I do not focus on the communicative competence of Brazilian immigrants in the Portuguese language.[25] Instead, I examine the possible social factors influencing the language

---

José Osvaldo de Araújo, Ana Carla França and Ana Paula França, *Brazilians in London: A Report for the 'Strangers into the Citizens' Campaign* (London: Department of Geography, Queen Mary, University of London, 2007).

[22] See online at <www.ibge.gov.br/brasil500/index2.html> for a summary of the history of immigration to Brazil between 1500 and 2000 [accessed 8 October 2009].

[23] Besides being advertised by the venues where the events take place, they are also found on the Brazilian Embassy webpage, <http://www.brazil.org.uk>.

[24] See the associations' websites online at www.abras.org.uk and www.abrir.org.uk for further information.

[25] Ana Beatriz Barbosa de Souza. '"Should I speak Portuguese or English?" Ethnic and social identity construction in the language choices of Brazilian mothers and their mixed-heritage

choices of families who are part of the literacy school organized by a group of Brazilian mothers, such as the influence of exogamy, the attitudes to the receptor and minority groups, trips to the homeland, the intention to return, the patterns of language use and the sense of ethnic identity.

The Participant Families

Since intermarriage is recognized as one of the main causes of minority group language loss,[26] I explore language issues in families where the mother is Brazilian and the father is of another nationality. Nine families which fit this criterion and whose children attend a Brazilian community language school in London were invited to participate in this project. The children were five to twelve years old and were selected from the three different Portuguese classes which the school ran at the time: stage 1 for children aged five to eight, focusing on the development of oral skills; stage 2 for children also aged five to eight who, now having oral skills, would develop literacy skills; and stage 3 for children aged eight to twelve, to develop their literacy skills even further.

A general profile of these families can be presented by drawing on certain social, cultural and linguistic factors that were identified by the mothers in their interviews for this study. With regards to social factors, the families taking part have an average of two children, and although their level of education varies, the majority of the parents have completed a university degree. Most of the mothers are self-employed, some working with other Brazilians resident in London (in the catering industry and translation services, for example), and some with the Brazilians who visit London for a short period of time (in the travel industry, for example, and providing interpretation services). All the fathers work and most of them are in the professional sector. The families do not live in one particular zone of London, and would consider themselves to be middle class.

With regards to cultural factors, these families confirm that they make considerable efforts to maintain links with Brazil: they do this not only by visiting the country on a regular basis, but also by building social network ties with other Brazilians in London, such as being affiliated to Brazilian political parties, attending Brazilian cultural events and being involved with the Brazilian community language school their children attend.

With regard to linguistic factors, the principal service sector used by these families which employs Portuguese as the main language of business is related to the sale of ethnic consumables, such as grocery shops, restaurants, bakeries and coffee houses. However, these families also use specialist travel agencies and

---

children, at home and in a community language school in the UK' (unpublished PhD thesis, University of Southampton, 2006).

[26] Tariq Modood, Richard Bethoud, Jane Lakly, James Nazroo, Patten Smith, Satnam Virdee and Saron Beishon, *Ethnic Minorities in Britain: Diversity and Disadvantage* (London: PSI, 1997).

consulate services, in which Portuguese is again the main language of business. The mothers have also established a friendship network in London, and the main language of communication between members is Portuguese. Most mothers also report using only Portuguese at home with their children and indicate that language is essential to the maintenance of their group identity, as illustrated by the responses below.

> Sou brasileira, não nasci aqui. Minha cultura é brasileira. Por isso, português é importante para meus filhos entenderem isso tudo.[27]
>
> [I am Brazilian, I was not born here. My culture is Brazilian. So, Portuguese is important for my children to understand all of this.]
>
> Português é a minha língua. E meus filhos são metade brasileiros. Então eu acho horrível quando alguém fala 'minha mãe é brasileira' mas eles não sabem falar uma palavra de português. Isso reflete em mim. Morro de vergonha![28]
>
> [Portuguese is my language. And my children are half-Brazilian. So, I find it terrible when someone says 'My mother is Brazilian' but they cannot say a word in Portuguese. It reflects on me. I feel so embarrassed!]
>
> Você não é brasileiro se não sabe falar português [...]. Não faz o menor sentido a mãe falar português e os filhos não.[29]
>
> [You are not Brazilian if you cannot speak Portuguese [...]. It makes no sense at all for the mother to speak Portuguese and the children not to.]

These statements show that these mothers' sense of ethnic identity can be related to their linguistic and cultural background and/or to their feelings of belonging to that ethnicity. Nevertheless, the mothers also report that they have practical reasons for ensuring that their children learn Portuguese. Firstly, there are the mothers' concerns regarding their children's professional future and the option of living and working in Brazil. Secondly, there is the pragmatic need to speak Portuguese to relatives living in Brazil.

The children seem to be conscious of the interactional necessity to be able to communicate in both Portuguese and English. Two mothers reported that their children had gone through a period in which they would speak one language (Portuguese) with adults and another (English) with other children. This example shows that the children look for linguistic patterns and feel motivated to use different languages according to the practical needs of the situation. The mothers also report that the choice between English and Portuguese is often related to expressing their emotional experiences, for themselves and for their children:

> Mostro minhas emoções quando falo português.[30]
>
> [I can show my emotions when I speak Portuguese.]

---

[27] Mother 1.
[28] Mother 2.
[29] Mother 3.
[30] Mother 4.

Meus filhos falam português com as pessoas que eles têm mais intimidade.[31]

[My children speak Portuguese to people they feel more intimate with.]

Through these interviews it becomes apparent that these mothers assigned huge importance to being able to converse in Portuguese as far as the maintenance of a Brazilian self-identification strategy is concerned. However, the question remains as to how these mothers' self-identification strategies impact on their children.

The Children

I now illustrate the impact of the mothers' self-identification on their children by focusing my discussion on the data provided by the three children who attended the community language school for the longest period of time: Josefa, Benedito and Antônio. These children, whose names have been changed to preserve their anonymity, were interviewed individually due to their different levels of competence in Portuguese, and their differing personalities and ages. Interviewing the children individually was also important in guaranteeing confidentiality, as well as avoiding peer pressure on their replies and language choices.

Josefa

Josefa is six years old and was born in London. She travels to Brazil once a year to visit family, and is communicatively competent in Portuguese and English. She and her mother live with a non-English-speaking Brazilian relative, which means that Portuguese is the predominant language of the home. Her father sees her regularly but speaks to her only in English. According to her mother, Josefa can read and write in both languages, but her literacy skills are better in English. She also states that her daughter speaks Portuguese to adults, reads comics and children's books in Portuguese and can recount Brazilian nursery rhymes and songs. Josefa attends the Brazilian cultural events organized by the community language school once a term.

In turn, Josefa (J) herself presented some interesting data. In the interview with the researcher (R), she applies criteria such as place of birth and language spoken to define ethnic identity:

> R: Como você sabe que ela é brasileira?
> J: Porque ela vive lá e ela tem passaporte brasileiro.
>
> [R: How do you know she's Brazilian?
> J: Because she lives there and she has got a Brazilian passport.]
>
> J: Tenho namorado.
> R: Ele é brasileiro ou inglês?
> J: Inglês.
> R: Como você sabe que ele é inglês?
> J: Porque ele não fala brasileiro.

[31] Mother 5.

[J: I have got a boyfriend.
R: Is he Brazilian or English?
J: He's English.
R: How do you know he's English?
J: Because he does not speak Brazilian.]

According to Hoffman, children from the age of 2 years and 10 months can attach language to different speakers.[32] In other words, children from that young age are aware of which language to use to which person, as acknowledged by Josefa in the extract below:

R: Você gosta de falar português com a [sua prima]?
J: Sim, porque se eu não falar português com [minha prima] ela não me entende. E porque eu fico muito com ela, eu falo português com a minha mãe também.

[R: Do you like speaking Portuguese to [your cousin]?
J: Yes, because if I didn't speak Portuguese to [my cousin] she wouldn't understand me. And because I stay with her a lot, I speak Portuguese to my mother as well.]

Josefa also appears to react positively to the use of both Portuguese and English:

R: Você gosta de falar português?
J: Sim, muito, muito, muito.
R: Você gosta de falar inglês?
J: Sim, muito também.
R: O que você fala mais, português ou inglês?
J: Português.

[R: Do you like speaking Portuguese?
J: Yes, a lot, a lot, a lot.
R: Do you like speaking English?
J: Yes, a lot as well.
R: Which one do you speak most, Portuguese or English?
J: Portuguese.]

Although she lives in England, attends the local state school, and always communicates in English with her father, Josefa reports that she speaks more Portuguese than English. One might consider that Josefa's answers could have been influenced by the fact that she is aware of my preference for Portuguese. However, her answers could also be a consequence of the fact that her mother, who self-identifies as a 'tourist', chooses to have more and stronger links to other Portuguese speakers, leading Josefa to be more exposed to Portuguese than English in her daily life.

Nevertheless, in an activity where she was asked to imagine that she had to speak to an alien, Josefa describes herself as English, which seems to be related to the fact that she was born in England:

---

[32] Charlotte Hoffman, 'Language Acquisition in Two Trilingual Children', *Journal of Multilingual and Multicultural Development*, 6 (1985), 479–95 (p. 483).

> R: (Daí ele pergunta), 'Josefa, de onde você é?'
> J: Sou da Inglaterra.
>
> [R: (Then he asks), 'Josefa, where are you from?'
> J: I'm from England.]

Despite being very clear about where she is from, the language factor seems to confuse Josefa in relation to her ethnic identity. In the extract below, Josefa starts to refer to the Portuguese language but changes her mind, apparently selecting English since it reflects her place of birth rather than ethnic identity:

> R: Josefa, que línguas você fala?
> J: (pause) Por... in-inglês.
> R: Você só fala inglês?
> J: E português.
>
> [R: (...asks) Josefa, which languages do you speak?
> J: (pause) Por... En-English.
> R: (...asks) Do you only speak English?
> J: And Portuguese.]

Although her mother's self-identity tends towards the 'tourist' end of the identity continuum, the adoption of objective criteria for defining ethnicity seems to undermine Josefa's reported positive attitudes towards speaking Portuguese. However, these positive attitudes towards Portuguese do seem to influence her language choice in the interview: when given the choice, Josefa insisted on using Portuguese with the researcher.

Benedito

Benedito is a six-year-old boy who was born in London. According to his mother, he understands, speaks, reads and writes both Portuguese and English and is used to conversing in both at home, where it is common to find other Brazilians staying for extended periods. Benedito has friends with whom he speaks Portuguese at his mainstream school and at the community language school he attends, and he plays an active part in the latter's cultural events. His mother has also encouraged him to read Portuguese language comic books and storybooks, and to recount Portuguese language nursery rhymes and songs.

Benedito appears to be fluent in Portuguese and states that he is happy to speak it, but subsequent comments indicate that this has not always been the case. He states clearly that as a very young child he did not like exchanges in Portuguese with his mother:

> Quando eu era pequeno, eu não sabia português e não gostava quando
> minha mãe falava comigo em português.
>
> [When I was small I didn't know Portuguese and I didn't like it when my
> mum spoke to me in Portuguese.]

Benedito suggests that this dislike of Portuguese was primarily related to the performative aspect of his competence in Portuguese, since he found it difficult to understand the language and to respond in it. However, his next comment indicates that this phase was short-lived; his improved abilities in the language increased his confidence in its use and hence, his attitude towards it:

> Quando eu tinha três anos, eu gostava quando minha mãe falava português comigo.
>
> [When I was three, I liked it when my mum spoke Portuguese to me.]

Despite having positive language attitudes towards speaking Portuguese, Benedito's ethnic identity as an English boy has not been affected. He self-identifies as English as a result of having been born in England:

> R: De onde você é?
> B: Sou — esqueci
>
> [R: Where are you from?
> B: I'm from — I forgot]
>
> R: (asks again in English) Where are you from?
> B: England.
> R: Como você sabe que você é inglês?
> B: Como eu sei? Porque eu nasci na Inglaterra.
>
> [R: How do you know you're English?
> B: How do I know? Because I was born in England.]

Benedito expresses positive attitudes to both languages which are part of his life as a consequence of being surrounded by supportive attitudes to his bilingualism:

> R: Mas você prefere falar português ou inglês?
> B: Português.
> R: Qual você acha mais fácil?
> B: Inglês. Qual você acha mais fácil?
>
> [R: But do you prefer speaking Portuguese or English?
> B: Portuguese.
> R: Which one do you find easier?
> B: English. Which one do you find easier?]

As mentioned above by Benedito himself, identity is not solely related to place of birth. According to him, there is also a relationship between identity and language spoken. Thus, as Benedito self-identifies as English, he first mentions speaking English and only then does he refer to being able to speak Portuguese:

> R: Que línguas você fala?
> B: Inglês e português.
>
> [R: What languages do you speak?
> B: English and Portuguese.]

In contrast to Josefa, who does not refer to her Portuguese speaking skills when defining her ethnic identity, Benedito mentions both languages when defining his own skills:

> R: Eu achava que você era brasileiro.
> B: (pause) Falo duas línguas.
>
> [R: I thought you were Brazilian.
> B: (pause) I speak two languages.]

Benedito expresses a preference for the use of Portuguese during the interview; however, this may have been based on his knowledge of the researcher's background rather than on any other attitudinal factor. This language choice also indicates that Benedito links languages to people. Benedito knows me from the Brazilian community language school where only Portuguese is spoken to the adults. Nevertheless, Benedito is aware that he would meet different people in the same places, leading him to use different languages in the same domain.

> Falo português com uma menina portuguesa na escola — Ela tem uma irmã brasileira também.
>
> [I speak Portuguese to a Portuguese girl at school — She has a Brazilian sister as well.]

Benedito is communicatively competent in Portuguese, as shown in his interview, and in English, as reported by his mother. Once again, his bilingual status appears to be a consequence of different factors. Firstly, Benedito's parents also used the one-parent, one-language strategy with their son, and secondly, there is an instrumental need to speak Portuguese to the many Brazilians who have lived in his house and who are part of his mother's social network. In addition, Benedito's mother has invested in his formal education in Portuguese by enrolling her son in both the European Portuguese and the Brazilian Portuguese community language schools. His father is English but he understands Portuguese and has travelled to Brazil with the family a couple of times. This contextual information offers a brief insight into the reasons why Benedito may express positive attitudes towards the use of the Portuguese language. Once again, he claims to enjoy the contact he has with Brazil and Brazilians; he also likes interacting in Portuguese and attending the community language schools.

Antônio

Antônio is a nine-year-old boy who was born and lives in London, although he did spend a year living in Brazil from the age of two, where he attended nursery school. Antônio demonstrates communicative competence in both Portuguese and English and his mother attests that he has sound reading and writing skills in both languages. However, English is the only language used in Antônio's home. His mother has actively decided not to raise her family in Portuguese, a choice she claims is to do with emotional links she has with English. However, she wants her son to learn Portuguese and gain an appreciation of Brazilian culture and literature, primarily for essentialist reasons to do with heritage, and for this reason Antônio attends a community language school.

Antônio has Brazilian and Portuguese friends with whom he converses in

Portuguese. He attends cultural events organized by the community language school and regularly visits his mother's Brazilian friends. Antônio's mother has also ensured that he has been exposed to Brazilian culture through nursery rhymes, music, children's stories and comic books.

In his own interview, Antônio talks about a friend of his; he refers to place of birth and parents' background as important constructs of this boy's identity:

> R: Mas como ele é inglês se a mãe dele não é?
> A: Porque o pai dele é inglês. Ele é metade inglês e metade brasileiro.
>
> [R: But how is he English if his mother isn't?
> A: Because his dad is English. He's half-English and half-Brazilian.]

Antônio uses the same criteria to define his own ethnic identity. In the activity where the children were asked to imagine talking about themselves to an alien, Antônio refers to being both English and Brazilian, as shown in the extract below:

> R: E se ele te perguntar quem você é?
> A: Sou Antônio. Tenho 9 anos. E gosto de esportes.
> R: E se ele te perguntar de onde você é?
> A: Falaria Inglaterra e Brasil.
> R: Os dois? Como você pode ser de dois lugares diferentes ao mesmo tempo?
> A: Minha mãe e meu pai. Minha mãe é brasileira e meu pai é inglês.
>
> [R: What if he asks who you are?
> A: I'm Antônio. I'm nine years old. And I like sports.
> R: What about if he asks where you are from?
> A: I would say England and Brazil.
> R: Both? How can you be from two different places at the same time?
> A: My mum and dad. My mum is Brazilian and my dad is English.]

However, language does not appear to be the core value of Antônio's ethnic identity. He emphasizes how he has inherited his sense of Brazilian culture from his parents, but he states that English is his preferred language and the one he uses more often:

> R: O que você falaria se ele te perguntasse que língua você fala?
> A: Inglês.
> R: Só?
> A: Falo português.
> R: Mas você não contaria pra ele?
> A: Contaria, mas eu geralmente falo inglês.
>
> [R: And what would you say if he asks you what language you speak?
> A: English.
> R: Only?
> A: I speak Portuguese.
> R: But you wouldn't tell him?
> A: I would, but I usually speak English.]

This sense of a stronger allegiance to Brazilian culture than to the language itself appears to be comparable to that expressed by his mother. Although her son demonstrates a high level of communicative competence in both Portuguese and English, his preference for English appears to be strongly related to finding it easier. English is also Antônio's choice of language in written exercises:

> R: Você quer que eu te ajude fazendo perguntas?
> A: (pause) Posso escrever em inglês?
> R: (nodding) Huh-huh.
>
> [R: Do you want me to help you [with this task] by asking you questions?]
> A: (pause) Can I write in English?
> R: (nodding) Huh-huh.]

However, Antônio is aware of the influence of context when choosing which of his languages to use within a particular domain. He is aware that English is not only his home language but the national language of England, but that at the community language school the language of use is Portuguese:

> R: Que língua você fala em casa?
> A: Inglês.
> R: Onde você fala português?
> A: Na escola aos sábados.
> R: Só lá?
> A: Sim.
>
> [R: Which language do you speak at home?
> A: English.
> R: Where do you speak Portuguese?
> A: At the school on Saturdays.
> R: Only there?
> A: Yes.]

Conclusions

Being born in Brazil and speaking Brazilian Portuguese as their first language allows the mothers to see themselves as Brazilians. This sense of identity is then affected in different degrees when they move to England and learn to speak English. The mothers' self-identities are only signposts in the identity continuum adopted in this study. The mothers' self-identification depends on how much their 'Brazilianness' is affected by the 'Englishness' of their experiences of living in London in different situations and at different times. In other words, the way the mothers self-identify is multiple, and changeable according to context. Nevertheless, the mothers' reports on the importance of ethnicity to their social identities were used as a general background to examine how their positioning impact on their children.

Josefa describes herself as English because she was born in England and because she speaks English. In spite of using Portuguese in her interview, she avoids referring to her ability in speaking this language when describing herself. This behaviour seems to signal her awareness of the fact that adding this criterion to her description would go against the characteristics she selected to describe others: place of birth and language spoken. Trying to adopt clear-cut criteria of ethnicity seems to be an influence of her mother, who tends to position herself towards the 'tourist' end of the identity continuum.

Benedito's self-identification strategies also appear to be influenced by those of his mother, who tends towards the 'expatriate cosmopolitan' end of the identity continuum. In other words, his mother is willing to adopt some of the characteristics from both the receptor (English) and the minority (Brazilian) groups. Nonetheless, she claims to feel Brazilian since she was born there and grew up there. In the same way that she is attached to her place of birth and the language of her childhood, Benedito appears attached to his place of birth (England) and the language which he first learned (English). He feels English, and as in the case of Josefa, the way he self-identifies appears to be related to the language he finds easier, uses more often and of which he has better knowledge. However, Benedito signals that, like his mother, he feels comfortable with adopting another language and other cultural experiences.

In contrast to both Josefa and Benedito, Antônio self-identifies as being both English and Brazilian in spite of having been born in England and having English as the language of his household. Antônio justifies this label by adding his parents' backgrounds to the set of criteria for determining his ethnic identity. The way Antônio self-identifies is an indication that his mother (who tends to place herself in the 'early cosmopolitan' identification category in the identity continuum) has influenced him. She self-identifies as being 'hybrid' but has strong links to English society and the English language. Despite demonstrating positive attitudes towards Brazilian culture and the Portuguese language, Antônio also has strong links to his English identity. Nevertheless, Antônio's mother seems to have been successful in highlighting the importance she gives to both identities in their lives.

Overall, the discussion in this article suggests that the way in which migrant mothers react to their contact with the receptor community influences their children's sense of ethnicity, and thus, their emotional and instrumental links to their community language.

GOLDSMITHS, UNIVERSITY OF LONDON

Family and Transmission: Collective Memory in Identification Practices of Madeirans on Jersey

VANESSA MAR-MOLINERO

Introduction

For the past fifty years many Portuguese have migrated to Jersey, mostly for economic reasons.[1] From the first arrivals in the 1950s of a few hundred seasonal workers, the number of Portuguese immigrants had grown by the beginning of the millennium to approximately 6000 people, according to official figures, accounting for some 6 per cent of the island's population.[2] Of this migratory group, mostly from the Madeiran archipelago, many have been on the island for substantial periods of time. Some have had children on the island, but many of the older migrants already had children whom they had left with members of the family on Madeira whilst they worked on Jersey; once settled, they brought their children over to join them, thus swelling the numbers of Portuguese speakers on the island. Given that very little research has been carried out on these populations, my own contribution seeks to fill some of the gaps in our knowledge by studying the children of the Madeiran migrants on Jersey, particularly with regard to identity construction, through a focus on the relationship between collective memory and identification.

Methodological Considerations

This study focuses primarily on the one-point-five and second generation Madeirans on Jersey,[3] and employs a range of different research methods. Primary data is gained through oral history techniques and ethnography, and is used alongside conventional secondary sources from archives and publications, as well as local and national newspapers, census data, government and non-governmental reports, and online sources.

---

[1] Jaine Beswick, 'The Portuguese Diaspora on Jersey', in *The Consequences of Mobility*, ed. by Bent Priesler and Anne Fabricius (Roskilde: Roskilde University, 2005), pp. 93–105. The reasons why the respondents of this study designate themselves 'Portuguese' or 'Madeiran' are not the focus of this essay, and for this reason I will use these terms interchangeably.

[2] Etat Civil Committee, *Report on the 2001 census Jersey* (October 2002), online at <http://www.gov.je/ChiefMinister/Statistics/census/> [accessed 14 November 2009]. However, the true figure is estimated to be much higher, as I discuss later.

[3] By one-point-five generation I refer to those migrants who were born in Madeira and brought over to Jersey to join their parents, whilst the second generation are those born on Jersey to Madeiran parents.

Fieldwork was primarily ethnographic, since considerable time was spent living with Portuguese residents as a participant observer. This process allowed me to create relationships of trust through my gatekeepers with my informants. As a consequence, in the interviews they were more willing to offer information about themselves, without the feeling that I was intruding on their personal lives in a negative manner. Furthermore, my informants were assured that any information used or quoted would be kept anonymous.

Through this methodology I was able to observe social interactions in home life, and in cafes, shops, and social gatherings on Jersey in order to gain the trust of those I came into contact with and also to gather further ethnographic data. A second fieldwork stage allowed me to return to stay with the same family, and during this period I conducted both individual and group interviews. All of the interviewees elected to be interviewed in English, although in some cases the conversations moved between Portuguese and English. Interviews primarily explored questions about the subject's lives, their families and their experiences of being either migrants or the children of migrants, which meant that the sequence of the interviews tended to be in the form of life stories. The interview methodology that I employed used open-ended questions in order to permit the informants to talk about and develop subjects and experiences that were important to them.

Theoretical Framework

In my analysis of this community,[4] I draw on the theoretical framework of memory studies. I start from Halbwachs's concept that memory can be seen to be constantly (re)formed through social interaction and therefore cannot be considered an objective or static, given concept that belongs only to the individual, but rather a continuously changing, socially constructed notion that includes others' memories and shared cultural codes.[5] Taking this to be the case, we may then view memory and our relationship with memory in the same light as the formation of our identity, because, according to Gillis, both are a form of shared subjectivity and 'are not things we think about, but things we think with. As such they have no existence beyond our politics, our social relations, and our histories.'[6]

---

[4] In this study I define community and the sense of community experienced in line with the literature of Anderson's 'imagined community' whereby one cannot know all the individuals of a community and therefore through shared imagined idea of what it is to belong to a certain group or nation we can imagine a communion of the people we share our nation with. Benedict Anderson, *Imagined Communities: Reflections on the Origin and Spread of Nationalism*, rev. edn (London and New York: Verso, 1991). See also Beswick and Pozo-Gutiérrez, and Sheringham, in this volume.

[5] Maurice Halbwachs, *On Collective Memory* [1925] (London: University of Chicago Press, 1992).

[6] *Commemorations: The Politics of National Identity*, ed. by John R. Gillis (Princeton, NJ: Princeton University Press, 1994), p. 52.

For example, the formation of our identities (gender, political, national, etc) can be seen as a continuous process of giving and taking that is constantly (re)creating group boundaries and the parameters of identity, because the subject endlessly sorts through features of identification such as events, places and persons that stress belonging to some groups and differentiation from others.[7]

However, these features of identification are not always linked to a subject's lived experience, but can also be conveyed through the memories of others within the parameters of the community and identification group. Thus, one of the ways in which both memory and identity can be seen to be entwined is by considering how subjects, in this case the one-point-five and second generation Madeirans, draw on a repository of collective memories to form a sense of belonging.

In order to evaluate to what extent the second and one-point-five generations share a collective memory, it was essential to consider the process of transmission. The transmission of collective memory can be viewed in the same terms as Billig's concept of 'banal' nationalism. Billig argues that nationalism is not on the periphery of people's lives but, rather, that citizens are reminded daily of their national place. These reminders are so familiar and ordinary that they are not 'consciously registered as reminding'.[8] This can also be applied to the ways in which we practise our collective identity, which are also extremely familiar and ordinary. For example, a person does not remember their birth nor are they believed to have many firm memories before the age of three. However, the collective members of their family do remember their birth and commemorate it each year in the form of a birthday. Consciously then, we are not aware of our birth, but the memory of it within the collective sphere is unquestioned and through repetition we too accept that one day of the year is our birthday.

Therefore, many forms of habitual, skilled remembering are used in our daily lives, from cooking to the naming of the objects we eat, each of which shows a linking with the past in the present, however ordinary and familiar these tasks of our everyday life may seem. The selection of the task and practices that we adopt within the different groups in our everyday life are the markers with which we form our identification with some groups and our lack of identification with others, as we partake in different groups with distinctive characteristics. In this paper I utilize this understanding of collective memory to frame the discussion and analysis of the Portuguese on Jersey.

Portuguese Migration to Jersey

Situated approximately one hundred miles south of England and within sight of the French coast, the island of Jersey is the largest of the Channel Islands. Jersey has a long history of immigration dating back to the Middle Ages. From the

---

[7] Michael Pollack, 'Memória e identidade social', *Estudos históricos*, 5, 10 (1992), 200–12.

[8] Michael Billig, *Banal Nationalism* (London: Sage Publications, 1995), p. 8.

nineteenth century until the Second World War, the agricultural sector relied heavily on Breton workers; over time, many of these workers became tenants and even owners of farms by marrying Jersey-born wives with the right to own property.[9] When the economy experienced a huge growth in the post-war period, the work of Breton migrants began to be taken over by Madeiran migrants.

Between 1950 and 1976, over 100,000 migrants would leave Madeira.[10] For most of the twentieth century, the Madeiran economy had been in dire straits, reliant primarily on subsistence farming; as a result, many Madeirans were living in abject poverty.[11] Jersey already had a long history of migrant workers, and in the 1960s a delegation from Jersey was sent to Madeira to 'invite' workers over to the island as seasonal labourers in the agricultural sector.[12] However, the Jersey post-war boom resulted in heavy investment in the tourist industry — Uttley records that in 1964 the number of visitors to the island rose above 500,000 for the first time, primarily as a result of the rise of the package holiday.[13] As a consequence, by the mid 1960s there was a pressing demand for skilled hotel and catering workers. By the late 1950s Portugal, and in particular Madeira, were already popular tourist destinations, meaning that a large pool of skilled hotel and catering workers already existed there, many of whom were tempted over by higher salaries and better work opportunities.[14] Thus, a combination of the presence of trained workers in Madeira, a need for such workers on Jersey, and a well-established tradition of emigration from Portugal to other European destinations meant that many Madeirans began to work on Jersey in the service sector.[15]

As was the case in many European countries at this time, working on Jersey required a work permit. Most permits were renewable every six months, which meant that the majority of Madeirans went to Jersey during the tourist season of April to October and returned to Madeira during the winter months. This often resulted in families being divided, with many parents leaving their children in Madeira with relatives, since the living conditions and hours they worked were inappropriate for children. In some circumstances, where employers could prove that there was need for a longer duration of stay, twelve-month permits were issued. In a small number of cases this meant that whole families could move to Jersey, although it was more common for wives to join their husbands than for children to be brought over. The law for Portuguese entrants to Jersey did

---

[9] Channel Islands Study Group, *Nos Iles: A Symposium on the Channel Islands* (Middlesex: CISG, 1944), p. 5.
[10] Jose Guerreiro, 'Análise Tendencial da Emigração Portuguesa nos Últimos Anos', in *Estudos sobre a Emigração Portuguesa*, ed. by Maria Beatriz Rocha-Trindade (Lisbon: Sá da Costa Editora, 1981), pp. 31–69 (p. 40).
[11] Beswick, p. 98.
[12] Beswick (personal communication).
[13] John Uttley, *The Story of the Channel Islands* (London: Faber and Faber, 1966), p. 215.
[14] Pathfinders, *The Portuguese World*, online at <http://www.bbc.co.uk/jersey/voices/pathfinders.shtml> [accessed 23 November 2009].
[15] Pathfinders (2000).

not change until Portugal became a full member of the EU, in 1992, allowing Madeirans to travel freely to Jersey and also to unite their families on the island.[16]

Before the 1970s, the number of Madeirans on Jersey is thought to have been in the hundreds. However, by 1975 there were over two thousand Portuguese people on Jersey.[17] This is a figure that has continued to rise over the years. Indeed, the 2001 census indicated that at the start of the new millennium more than 5500 people of Portuguese extraction were living on the island, constituting 6 per cent of the total population.[18] Although the Portuguese are now the second largest migrant community on Jersey (the first being immigration from the UK), they are not mentioned in any of the tourist guides, or social, political or historical writings of the Island. With regard to the latter three topics, Beswick notes that in point of fact, very little is written concerning any period after the German occupation during the Second World War, and concludes that 'Portuguese emigration to the Island is not discussed, if alluded to at all in figures'.[19]

The only official statistics regarding the Portuguese on Jersey are to be found in the census data, the most recent being that of 2001.[20] The census data is interesting in itself as there are disparities between those born in Portugal, those who believe themselves to have a Portuguese cultural and ethnic background, and those who speak Portuguese either as their first or second language (see Table 1). The official figure used by the States of Jersey for the size of the Portuguese community is 6 per cent. This reflects the 5137 people born in Portugal. Nevertheless, the figure for those who believe themselves to have a Portuguese cultural or ethnic background is 5548, which suggests that there are an extra 411 people not born in Portugal who consider themselves to be Portuguese. This increases the total figure for the community to 6.4 per cent and possibly reflects second-generation Portuguese who do not consider themselves to be of Jersey cultural or ethnic background.[21] We must also take into consideration the discrepancies between the number of Portuguese-born and the number of first- and second-language speakers of Portuguese on the island. Of the 5137 people born in Portugal only

---

[16] Beswick, p. 98. For a more general account of Portuguese migratory patterns in the 1990s, see Martin Eaton, 'Immigration in the 1990s: A Study of the Portuguese Labour Market', *European Urban and Regional Studies*, 6, 4 (1999), 364–70.

[17] Pathfinders (2000).

[18] Legacies, *Immigration and Emigration. Jersey: A State of Isolation* (2007) <http://www.bbc.co.uk/legacies/immig_emig/channel_islands/jersey/article_4.shtml> [accessed 14 November 2009].

[19] Beswick, p. 97.

[20] Etat Civil Committee, *Report on the 2001 census Jersey* (see note 2).

[21] To overcome the issues posed by use of 'ethnicity' as a homogenous form, I adopt the strategy of Chris Barker and Dariusz Galasinski, *Cultural Studies and Discourse Analysis: A Dialogue on Language and Identity* (London: Sage, 2001), who state that ethnicity deals with a local context rather than a 'blanket characteristic'. See also Ulrike Hanna Meinhof and Dariusz Galasinski, *The Language of Belonging* (Basingstoke: Palgrave Macmillan, 2005) (p. 17), who also suggest that there is no homogenous ethnicity at the national level, such as we may call Britishness in the approach of this essay. Instead, Meinhof and Galasinski see ethnicity as rooted in the local community, and intertwined with narratives such as age, class and gender.

	Population	Percentage
Place of Birth Portugal	5137	6%
Portuguese cultural or ethnic background	5548	6.4%
Portuguese main language	4002	8.4%
Portuguese second language	3303	

TABLE 1: The Portuguese community on Jersey
All statistics are taken from Etat Civil Committee (October 2002)

4002 consider Portuguese to be their first language, a figure that may reflect the fact that many one-point-five generation Portuguese now regard English as their main language. In addition, another 3303 people consider Portuguese to be their second language. There are therefore 7305 people who speak Portuguese, either as a first or second language, compared to 5548 people who regard themselves as being of a Portuguese cultural or ethnic background, a body of some 1757 people. This latter number is unlikely to refer to Channel Islanders, as Portuguese is not offered to them in any educational institution.[22] Therefore, it may be that in fact 8.4 per cent of the population of Jersey has some kind of Portuguese connection.

The Portuguese population of Jersey is spread out across the island, with some families living in rented accommodation on farms, although the area most densely populated by the Portuguese is within the more built-up areas of the main city, St Helier. Whilst the Portuguese are omitted from official documents, such as the history of the island or visitors' guides, they are very visible in everyday Jersey life. For example, within the centre of St Helier there are two small Portuguese supermarkets that sell everything from Portuguese speciality foods to ketchup imported from Portugal; two Portuguese coffee shops that also sell Portuguese cakes and run a parcel delivery service to and from Portugal; and at least two Portuguese restaurants that not only sell Portuguese food but also imported beers, wines and fruit juices. Furthermore, there is a Portuguese club; a Portuguese travel and employment agency; a Portuguese football team in the Jersey football league; a special service in the main Catholic Church in Portuguese and lessons for confirmation in Portuguese. Moreover, the Jersey government offers information in Portuguese, as does the hospital and the Citizens Advice Bureau. The largest supermarket on the island, the Co-op, even sells Portuguese magazines and books.

An important feature is the after-school club that was created to allow children with a Portuguese background to be able to take qualifications in the Portuguese language at GCSE level. These classes take place after school hours and are

---

[22] Beswick (personal communication) reports that the first, one-point-five and second generation Portuguese on the island are now unofficially believed to make up around 10 per cent of the total population.

not part of the mainstream curriculum, nor are children without a Portuguese background generally allowed to participate.[23] Portuguese A/AS level was until recently offered at two colleges, but the uptake was poor. A substantial proportion of Portuguese students do not achieve their potential at school. As the 2001 census reports states:

> Residents born in Portugal (including Madeira) had the largest proportion with no academic qualifications; the proportion of 88 per cent was approximately three times that of all other places of birth combined (29 per cent).[24]

Although this figure will account for a proportion of the one-point-five generation Portuguese, it does not include the second generation, as all the statistics in the census are considered by place of birth rather than ethnic and cultural background.

Whilst some Portuguese have prospered on Jersey, the majority are still involved in semi-skilled or working-class, low-paid jobs such as catering, agriculture, the hotel industry, cleaning and care.[25] Even though the Portuguese no longer need work permits, employers are required by law of the States of Jersey to attempt to fill positions with local people who have lived on the island for five consecutive years, and only if such a person is not found can they apply for a licence that enables them to employ a newcomer. However some industries, such as tourism and agriculture, have blanket licences to employ those who have been on the island for less than five years.[26]

The main theme that arose consistently in conversation with the one-point-five and second generation Madeirans was the importance of the role that their families played, not only their sense of who they were and who they wanted to be, but also in the ways in which they viewed the concept of 'home'. As a result, this paper will look at the process of identity construction and transmission within the family, the creation of a sense of belonging within the group, and the static and utopian vision of 'home' that was portrayed by my informants regarding Madeira.

---

[23] Beswick, p. 98.
[24] Etat Civil Committee, p. 58.
[25] Guida de Abreu and Hannah Lambert, *Final Report of 'The Education of Portuguese Students in English and Channel Island Schools' Project* (2003), online at <http://psych.brookes.ac.uk/portuguese/report/> [accessed 15 October 2009] (p. 284).
[26] Jersey Citizens Advice Bureau, *Information for those wishing to live and work in the Island* (Document 3.1.2 Jersey, 2007), online at <http://www.cab.org.je/index.php?option=com_content&task=view&id=91&Itemid=48> [accessed 5 June 2007].

The Family and Identity Transmission[27]

In the past, many European and Asian societies brought their children up to worship their family ancestors using shrines and other religious practices. Although this is not the case today, in many communities the family is still believed to be the central focus for the transmission of many markers of identity such as language, names, social standing, religion, social values and aspirations, fears, world views, and ways of behaving. In his article on the role of family in the construction of individuals' life stories, Thompson suggests that who we become, both personally and socially, is generally rooted in our families' own life experiences and narratives.[28] This theme often arose during my interviews. One of my respondents (A) told me:

> It's not where you're born. It's where your parents come from that matters, it's where your roots are: that's what makes you Portuguese.[29]

The patterns of transmission from the parents to my informants of their Portuguese identity within the private sphere of their houses was most obvious when they spoke about food and supporting a football team. The choice of supporting a Portuguese football team rather than a British team, something of concern mostly to male respondents, was influenced by their fathers. In the majority of households this was for one principal reason, namely the presence of Portuguese cable television in their homes. (B) stated that he supported Sporting Lisbon, a Portuguese football team, because

> When we're at home, my dad, he watches Portuguese cable, if you want to watch anything that's not Portuguese you gotta get a TV for your room, so we watch it with him like being at the game. So I don't watch English footy. Even when I go out it's to Portuguese clubs so the footy is also Portuguese.[30]

Most of my female interviewees were not interested in football. Instead they tended to talk more about the importance of the role that the family played in food choices and cooking. This was a topic that frequently came up in conversation with female informants. An example can be seen in the case of (C) who explained that when she lived at home she regularly went shopping with her parents to Portuguese shops. The reason for shopping at these locations was to buy Portuguese ingredients that were not available in the Jersey supermarkets.

---

[27] It is important to mention here that due to strict housing regulations on the island of Jersey the vast majority of my respondents still lived with their parents or extended families even though they ranged between the ages of 18 and 29.
[28] Paul Thompson, 'Family Myth, Models, and Denials in the Shaping of Individual Life Paths' in *Between Generations: Family Models, Myths and Memories*, ed. by Daniel Bertaux and Paul Thompson (London: Transaction Publishers, 1993), pp. 13–38 (p. 13).
[29] Interview with (A), Madeiran male, St Helier, 2 April 2007.
[30] Interview with (B), Madeiran male, St Helier, 1 April 2007.

When asked what types of food she cooked now that she did not live at home she replied:

> I cook a lot of Portuguese food [...] in fact I don't think I do anything English. If you get married you need to know how to cook so I learnt from my mum which means I learnt to cook Portuguese food.[31]

This represents an obvious transmission of gender roles within the family, although it is beyond the scope of this study. However, one male informant did comment on this, stating:

> I find more cultural differences in the way we were brought up compared to people here, you know, like in the way of women and men and what their duties are.[32]

The transmission of the family's values in terms of gendered roles also meant that many of my informants were adamant that if they were to get married it would be to another Portuguese person, since they would behave and react in the same manner, having been brought up in the same sociocultural and ethnic context.

All the informants stressed that their family friends were Portuguese and that socializing on Jersey took the form of Portuguese gatherings at physical locations that they deemed Portuguese, such as restaurants and clubs. This emphasizes the point that the immediate family within the private sphere may have promoted identification with being Portuguese at home. This was then acted out and practised in the public sphere among those whom parents considered kin and part of their community. One informant stated that it was difficult to tell that they were living on Jersey, especially when in the private sphere:

> Every minute I spent at home was like being over there [Madeira]. They didn't have any English friends until I was older than ten.[33]

She then went on to explain that when they entered the house they were expected by their father to speak in Portuguese so as 'not to forget who they were'. This was an aspect of home life that many of my informants commented on. For example, when they crossed the threshold of their houses their parents expected them to act out 'being Portuguese' by using the language and not behaving as they would at their 'English friends' houses'. By distinguishing the differences between themselves and outsiders, such as English friends, the parents of my informants were further reinforcing their identities as Portuguese and reminding their children that, as part of the family, they too were a part of this broader group.

Within the family system many myths and models are transmitted that shape the formation of one's identity.[34] For the people interviewed these models and myths were the sociocultural anchors that they believed made them Portuguese:

---

[31] Interview with (C), Madeiran female, St Helier, 5 April 2007.
[32] Interview with (D), Madeiran male, St Helier, 29 March 2007.
[33] Interview with (E), Madeiran female, St Helier, 29 March 2007.
[34] Bertaux and Thompson, eds, p. 37.

family gatherings, the food they ate, and religion. Family gatherings were typically described as being 'traditional'. This also meant that extended family and friends would be present and would partake in what were referred to as 'Portuguese stuff'.[35] In the winter this entailed gathering round the table to eat traditional meals such as the ubiquitous *bacalhau* (dried salted cod), to play cards and drink *Macieira*, a popular Portuguese brandy. During the summer, days would be set aside for barbecues:

> Like, in the summer, we have loads of barbecues with family and friends, Portuguese friends, and we always have *espetada* [barbecued skewered meat]. We spend, like, the whole afternoon and we, like, drink Portuguese drinks like *Sumol* and *laranjada* [fizzy drinks] and *Super Bock*, the Portuguese beer. All that stuff you can buy here; it's like being back in Madeira.[36]

When I asked if English people were invited to these gatherings, (G) explained that he had once invited his English girlfriend but that she had not enjoyed it because they were not like English barbecues:

> We don't just get pissed and eat burgers. Plus it's loads of different ages, you know. I don't mind havin' my little cousins around, and my family, like uncles and stuff, we're closer than English people, they're like friends. You know, she didn't speak Portuguese so she didn't understand stuff, like the family stories, didn't like the food, she's just not the same as us, better to keep it separate, you know.

These gatherings are the way in which the families' Portuguese practices are promoted and maintained. The function of remembering these practices and retelling family stories upholds commitment to the group at these meetings by symbolizing values, traditions and aspirations that constantly remind them of their Portuguese roots. Halbwachs states that even though we participate in events as individuals, our memories remain collective and attached to that group, because not only do our ideas originate from within it, but our thinking and actions keep us in contact with the group.[37] An example of this can be seen in the conversation I had with (H), who explained to me why she considered herself a Catholic, yet referred to herself as non-religious:

> Portuguese people are Catholic, like, all of us in one way or another, it's just part of being Portuguese; doesn't mean you practise, just your family are, so you are.[38]

She also explained that there was a French Catholic church on Jersey that had a Portuguese priest who celebrated Mass in Portuguese and also offered communion classes in Portuguese.[39] All my informants had attended this church at least once,

---

[35] Interview with (F), Madeiran male, St Helier, 29 March 2007.
[36] Interview with (G), Madeiran male, St Helier, 28 March 2007.
[37] Halbwachs, p. 23.
[38] Interview with (H), Madeiran female, St Helier, 2 April 2007.
[39] Portuguese mass is no longer conducted by a Portuguese priest, however. Instead, the local (English-speaking) Catholic priest conducts the Mass (still well attended), by reading a

and many commented that their parents had sent them to communion classes. All the one-point-five and second generation, even if they were not practising Catholics, referred to themselves as being Catholics as this was a significant marker in their Portuguese identity, inherited from their Portuguese parents. Rapport and Dawson underline the family's influence on such matters, stating that the family may be seen as a reference point for who we think we are, which means we identify and act out similarities within our group and, in doing so, create differences from the 'others'.[40]

One of the most notable ways in which informants believed that they were different from Jersey people was how they had been brought up by their parents. Many believed that the 'Portuguese way' of being brought up was a much harder and tougher upbringing than that of their Jersey counterparts, but that it taught them to respect their elders and to work hard. (I) continuously compared his upbringing to that of the Jersey children around him, concluding that:

> Jersey is different, on Jersey they bring their kids up different, they smoke, drink, swear, and don't respect their parents. You don't hear of Portuguese kids who don't respect their parents![41]

When informants were asked in what ways it was a tougher upbringing, many spoke about how strict their parents were. For example, as school children, none of them had been allowed to stay at English friends' houses even though sleepovers were a very common social practice amongst them. (J) explained that it was common for Portuguese children to have to be home by mealtime at seven o'clock in the evening, and that after dinner it was customary to spend time with the family because the Portuguese are more 'family oriented'.[42] (I) claimed to be able to identify a fellow Portuguese from their family's behaviour because 'every Portuguese family is the same over here, same fussing, same strict upbringing'.[43] Moreover (J) stated that although her parents were strict, this was not a huge issue since as she got older, she was able to go out with her parents:

> If I wanted to go out to a night club I would go with my mum and dad, it sounds kind of weird and controlling, but it was fun. We would go to the Portuguese Night and then my friends would also be there with their parents.

Portes, Fernandez-Kelly and Haller state that parental control when not in their home country normally disintegrates very fast as it is constantly challenged by unusual lifestyles, media-driven consumerism and peer influences.[44] Nonetheless,

---

prepared script written in Portuguese, even though his knowledge of the language is, by his own admission, poor (Beswick, personal communication).

[40] Nigel Rapport and Andrew Dawson, *Migrants of Identity* (Oxford: Berg, 1998), p. 142.
[41] Interview with (I), Madeiran male, St Helier, 2 April 2007.
[42] Interview with (J), Madeiran female, St Helier, 1 April 2007.
[43] Interview with (I), Madeiran male, St Helier, 2 April 2007.
[44] Alejandro Portes, Patricia Fernández-Kelly and William J. Haller, 'Segmented Assimilation on the Ground: The New Second Generation in Early Adulthood', *Ethnic and Racial Studies*, 28, 6 (2005), 1000–40 (p. 1013).

they also stress that the exception to this pattern is when the parents' expectations are reinforced by others in the community. Therefore, by mixing with other Portuguese families, the parents are integrating their children into the wider Portuguese community on Jersey, which helps to further establish their group identity as being Portuguese from the perspective both of the private and the public sphere.

Home and the Family

Whilst the role of the family in the creation of identification patterns is highly significant, because it defines where one belongs within a social framework, another key aspect is that of where one belongs physically. For the respondents, the concept of 'home' was one that they found hard to define. Many would comment that although they lived on Jersey with their families and for this reason would call the house in which they lived 'home', they also thought of Madeira as home. The naming of both places as home can be seen through the influence of the family, as according to Oakley 'the home is the family [... and] "home" and "family" are now virtually interchangeable terms'.[45] Thus, where the family physically lives at one moment in time is home, but equally the transmission by the parents of their sense of home as being Madeira has been passed on to the one-point-five and second generation to establish a dual sense of home.

Furthermore, in traditional definitions the concept of 'home' was as a physical aspect of one's life and could easily be interchanged with that of the house. More recently, however, commentators have considered home as something 'plurilocal'.[46] In an era of people migrating, travelling, being exiled or simply commuting, home is found within practised routines, myths, memories and repetitions of habitual interactions and 'stories carried around in one's head'.[47] Robins also stresses this point, depicting home as 'the driving imperative to salvage centred and coherent identities — placed identities for placeless times'.[48] Therefore, it is important to consider how parents have transmitted to their children a sense of Madeira as being their home that has subsequently forged an essential part of their identification within their family and community.

Of the respondents taking part in this study, fourteen had physical homes in Madeira that their parents had built whilst living and working on Jersey, and to which their parents intended to return to one day. Although some of these families have lived on Jersey for thirty years, the parents do not talk of it as home but, rather, strongly believe that eventually they will return to Madeira. (F) for example commented:

[45] Ann Oakley, *Housewife* (Harmondsworth: Penguin, 1976), p. 65.
[46] Roger Rouse, 'Mexican Migration and the Social Space of Postmodernism', *Diaspora*, 1, 1 (1991), 8–23 (p. 8).
[47] John Berger, *And Our Faces, My Heart, Brief as Photos* (London: Writers and Readers 1984), p. 64.
[48] Kevin Robins, 'Tradition and Translation: National Culture in its Global Context', in *Enterprise and Heritage: Crosscurrents of National Culture*, ed. by John Corner and Sylvia Harvey (London: Routledge, 1991), pp. 21–44 (p. 41).

> For as long as I can remember they have talked about goin' back, yeah but for what? They spend their lives workin' for a bloody house that's never used and then we live in a shit hole here. I don't see the point.[49]

The parents' efforts to keep this self-deception of eventual return alive can be seen through Freudian theory as a failure to work through the loss of an object. Working through is 'the process through which [one] accepts and incorporates an interpretation, overcoming the resistance it evokes'.[50] Thus working through and acting out can be seen as coexisting forces because the subject must face the threat that the process of working through may awaken a sense of betrayal and a feeling of weakening towards the lost object. In this case, Madeira as 'home' may be seen as the lost object. Hence, according to Freudian theory, the parent needs to work through the feelings of loss towards the homeland so as to be able to become part of Jersey society. However, instead of working through, the first generation have continued the phase of acting out. This has been done by building homes and creating a utopian and static vision of their homeland which is constantly recalled.

So great is the significance of the memory of the homeland for the parents that it has been transmitted from generation to generation, shaping the identity of the children. Hence, when the respondents were asked to recall what Madeira was like, not one commented on the high levels of unemployment or crime which were the original reasons which led their parents to leave the island, but instead their answers would always be positive and almost poetic. For example, (K) averred:

> The people are nicer, 'cos the place is so beautiful. You know you look up to these amazing mountains and down to the sea and the most perfect beaches. People are laid back; they have fun, it's different from here, like better.[51]

Yet earlier, (K) had been talking about his parents' move to Jersey, and he had described the hardship and poverty in which they had lived in Madeira. Hirsch and Spitzer refer to similar examples of generational transmission of memory as 'postmemory': a secondary, delayed memory mediated by stories, images and behaviours that are experienced through childhood, which then forms a 'mediated memory of a lost world of yesterday'.[52] This 'postmemory' is therefore not their own, but rather, one that one-point-five and second generation migrants have inherited from their parents and family.

---

[49] Interview with (F), Madeiran male, St Helier, 27 March 2007. In point of fact (F) is not questioning the 'sense of home' espoused by his parents, but rather alluding to the need to invest money to improve their material circumstances on Jersey.

[50] Sigmund Freud, *Mourning and Melancholia* [1917] (London: Penguin, 1991), pp. 251–68 (p. 252).

[51] Interview with (K), Madeiran male, St Helier, 29 March 2007.

[52] Marianne Hirsch and Leo Spitzer, 'We Would Never Have Come Without You: Generations of Nostalgia', in *Contested Pasts: The Politics of Memory*, ed. by Katherine Hodgkin and Susannah Radstone (London: Routledge, 2003), pp. 79–96 (p. 81).

Longing for the homeland, as seen above, has often been considered a form of nostalgia, either in its original meaning of 'homesickness' or the more recent definition of nostalgia as an 'inner space of psychic and emotional resonance'.[53] Valis considers that within all nostalgic constructions there must be a longing for a home 'that no longer exists or has never existed'.[54] As a result, although nostalgia can be said to be the product of something that 'once possessed detail, a specific shape, time and place' which can be recognized as being lost — for example, one's home — the effects of nostalgia dematerialize the object and it becomes a myth, such as everyone always being friendly in Madeira. Barthes describes myth as 'constituted by the loss of the historical quality of things', so that one loses a sense of what is historical reality affected by time and change and creates a static vision of the homeland.[55] Muñoz sees this as a 'ghost reality' where one does not realize or accept the present dynamic,[56] and for this reason, many of the respondents would not criticize any aspect of Madeiran life.

Another aspect fundamental to the construction of identity is that of landscapes. Although identity can be located in a physical landscape, imaginary landscapes are also highly significant. For my subjects, imagined images of their parents' lost homeland had been passed down through the generations and had summoned loyalties to Madeira and a sense of nostalgia. Hodgkin and Radstone comment that at times this may be such an influential identification that not only is nostalgia developed for their parents' lost physical landscape, but that it may create a need for the person to return to reclaim this landscape.[57] This was the case for many of the respondents in this study:

> I've never lived in Madeira, so kind of I can't say it's home 'cos I never lived there [...] but, yeah, I've lived in this house on Jersey like eight to nine years, so I kind of have to call it home, but a few months in Madeira in my house, well my dad's house, and with my people and my view of the sea, then that would be home, no question, yeah, definitely, no questions asked, one day I, like, go live back there.[58]

When the respondents were asked how they knew what Madeira was like, although they would say they had been on holiday to visit family there, their first answer was always 'from my parents'. Some felt compelled to prove that Madeira was beautiful and produced photographic evidence to that effect, depicting in particular family life. For example (L) stated that:

---

[53] Noël Valis, 'Nostalgia and Exile', *Journal of Spanish Cultural Studies*, 1, 2 (2000), 117–33 (p. 117).
[54] Valis, p. 131.
[55] Roland Barthes, *Mythologies*, trans. by Annette Lavers (New York: Hill and Wang, 1987), p. 131.
[56] Liliana Muñoz, 'Exile as Bereavement: Socio-Psychological Manifestations of Chilean Exiles in Great Britain', *British Journal of Medical Psychology*, 53, 3 (1980), 227–32 (p. 227).
[57] Hodgkin and Radstone, eds, p. 12.
[58] Interview with (F), Madeiran male, St Helier, 27 March 2007.

FIG. 1. An 'idyllic' landscape of Madeira

> My mum and dad always talked about Madeira, had photos of Madeira and the family, them when they were young. Like our family albums are all of Madeira [...] in fact even here [in the flat] I don't think I have one photo of Jersey. They are all of Madeira, now Mum has moved back with my boys, she sends me photos, so they're Madeira too.[59]

Hirsch views family photographs as a means of displaying the cohesion of the family. She explains that this is because they are able to give 'the illusion of being a simple transaction of the real' and therefore help to 'perpetuate familial myths'.[60] The photographs in (L)'s apartment were of the family standing at major sites in Madeira, for example, at the top of the highest mountain, or having barbecues in the forest. Moreover, the photographs her mother had sent her of her own children also tended to be in similar places and circumstances, which not only reinforces the image of the togetherness of the family but also of the idyllic landscapes of Madeira. Consequently, whilst many of the informants may have visited Madeira on holiday, they would only have seen the idyllic lifestyle of

---
[59] Interview with (L), Madeiran female, St Helier 28 March 2007.
[60] Marianne Hirsch, *Family Frames* (Cambridge, MA: Harvard University Press, 1997), pp. 8–9.

sightseeing or going to the beach; from the photographs this vision is increased and then reinforced by their parents' nostalgic images, which they themselves have then inherited. Furthermore, although the one-point-five generation lived in Madeira, they left at a very young age; nearly all were between eight and ten when they arrived on Jersey and thus:

> Couldn't bloody remember much, just like what my grandparents said. Like, going back helped loads, 'cos then I could see the school and think, yeah, I did this but if I didn't have my family to talk to about it, it'd probably just stay in my head.[61]

For one informant the creation of a static idyllic vision of her homeland has in fact been the reason that she has not returned to live in Madeira. (M) still remembers her life in Madeira before she left to live on Jersey, but over the years has begun to realize that these memories are not associated with the place she now visits on holiday.[62] Once she realized that she no longer knew people there, and that Madeira had changed from what she thought it was like, she had 'worked through', and refrained from acting out the nostalgic need to return, and had, instead, decided that Jersey was now her home:

> You grow up and your kind of attitudes to the memories you had of growing up there, things we would do, places, food and then realize that, well, that you don't actually know anyone there. I've got no friends there now, it's, like, I go over there now and I'm a stranger and I'm either with my parents or with Portuguese friends from Jersey that have gone over at the same time as me to visit. — Um, yeah, so I actually went there, and normally, you know, I come back [to Jersey] and I'd be crying like, oooh, what am I goin' to Jersey for, but actually last time I actually thought, no, I'm goin' home, to friends and work and stuff. So I guess, yeah, Jersey is home for me now.

Conclusions

As a result of the impact of the large Portuguese immigrant population, significant changes have occurred on Jersey at the political, social, economic and demographic levels, so that the topic of immigration is not only a political issue, but also a topic that is cutting across all dimensions of contemporary Jersey society. The main findings regarding identity and its rooting in the receptor or the home culture was mixed. Due to a combination of discrimination and their parents' nostalgia, the subjects have forged stronger identities with their Portuguese culture. However, they often comment that they are 'from nowhere'. One respondent stated that this has created a huge dilemma in her life. Although she identifies with the Portuguese community on Jersey, she neither feels accepted in Madeira nor in mainstream Jersey society:

---

[61] Interview with (B), Madeiran male, St Helier, 1 April 2007.
[62] Interview with (M), Madeiran female, St Helier, 1 April 2007.

> When I'm with my Portuguese friends in Madeira they call me *inglesa* which is, like, English girl, um, but when I'm with English people over here, I'm more of a Portuguese person to them... it's weird. I'm neither one nor the other.[63]

The complex issue of identification for the one-point-five and second-generation Portuguese has been highly influenced by the collective memory that they share with their family and the wider Portuguese community. The concept of 'not being from anywhere' highlights not only the element of rootless nostalgia for Madeira created through the inheritance of their family's collective memory, but also the insecurity that they feel towards any form of identification with the Jersey people.

Thanks are due to the Instituto Camões, which partially funded this research with a postgraduate student bursary.

UNIVERSITY OF SOUTHAMPTON

---

[63] Interview with (J), Madeiran female, St Helier, 1 April 2007.

Nas Terras de Sua Majestade: Portuguese Emigrants to Britain in the Works of Maria Ondina Braga

CLAIRE WILLIAMS

Introduction

Marina Lewycka's 2007 novel *Two Caravans* describes the adventures of idealistic migrant workers from Africa, Eastern Europe, Portugal and Brazil in the strawberry fields, battery farms, factories and cafés of twenty-first-century Britain.[1] The English characters represented are nothing like the bowler-hatted businessman Mr Brown and the housewife Mrs Brown about whom the Ukrainian protagonists have read in their English language textbooks, nor do there seem to be many of the other stereotyped fantasy British citizens: blonde bombshells with Ferraris and dashing men bearing Milk Tray chocolates. In fact, the immigrants have very little to do with the natives in general and more to do with abusive gangmasters and euphemistically self-designated 'recruitment consultants'. Her novel portrays through immigrant eyes the resulting culture clash between hopeful but stereotyped dreams and the disappointing and often dangerous reality. This is something that we can also see, although rarely, in Portuguese literary accounts of their visits to Britain.

The Portuguese have been migrating around the world for centuries, often writing up their impressions of weird and wonderful exotic cultures. Eça de Queirós and Ramalho Ortigão described nineteenth-century Britain with acuity, and a mixture of approval and criticism.[2] At the end of Chapter VI of *John Bull: depoimento de uma testemunha ácerca de alguns aspectos da vida e da civilisação ingleza* (1887), Ramalho Ortigão reported on the extremes of the social scale: in London, in the same day, one can see the Prince of Wales and the most wretched beggar, the Alpha and Omega of the human species.[3] Eça's portrayal of England in *Os Maias*, and his creation of stock characters Miss Jane, the perverse governess, and John Brown, the energetic Scots tutor to Carlos da Maia, laid the basis for many

---

[1] Marina Lewycka, *Two Caravans* (London: Fig Tree/Penguin, 2007).

[2] Nineteenth-century Portuguese impressions and literary expressions of England by Eça, Ramalho and Jaime Batalha Reis have been studied in detail in works such as Teresa Pinto Coelho, *A agulha de Cleópatra: Jaime Batalha Reis e as relações diplomáticas e culturais luso-britânicas* (Lisbon: Cosmos, 2000) and Américo Guerreiro de Sousa, *Inglaterra e França n'«Os Maias»: idealização e realidade* (Lisbon: Caminho, 2002).

[3] José Duarte Ramalho Ortigão, *John Bull: depoimento de uma testemunha ácerca de alguns aspectos da vida e da civilisação ingleza* (Porto: Lugan & Genelioux, 1887).

myths about Victorian England that are still taken seriously today, such as the fog in London, harsh educational measures and a hypocritical Puritanism masking licentious desires.[4]

Moving into the twentieth century, a number of Portuguese artists and writers came to London and settled here. These included, most famously, artists Paula Rego and Bartoloméu dos Santos, and poets Alberto Lacerda and Luís Amorim de Sousa (who has a collection entitled *Londres e Companhia*),[5] but also the numerous writers who came to this country as *leitores*, lecturers or postgraduate students: Helder Macedo, novelist and formerly Camões Professor at King's College, London (KCL), novelist Alexandre Pinheiro Torres who pioneered Luso-African literary studies in Cardiff, Américo Guerreiro de Sousa in Sheffield, José Cardoso Pires, Olga Gonçalves, Maria Velho da Costa and Gastão Cruz, also at KCL, Luís Miguel Nava in Oxford, and many more. Very few of them wrote about the experience of living in Britain, although Maria Velho da Costa published a series of chronicles, later collected in *O Mapa Cor de Rosa* (1984),[6] which show a London full of punks and tramps, but beautiful parks. Helder Macedo's novels *Partes de África* (1991), *Pedro e Paula* (1998), *Vícios e Virtudes* (2000) and *Sem Nome* (2005) all play on the overlapping of truth and fiction and include characters whose lives are remarkably similar, one assumes, to his own.[7] Thus they describe specific cafés in London, the life of a university lecturer, the Portuguese community in London, the difficulties of getting through customs, and so on. But this is largely to situate the narrator outside the main plot and give him the illusion of impartiality and his tale a flavour of authenticity.

Maria Ondina Braga's Life, Travels and Autobiographical Writing

The author I would like to focus on here, Maria Ondina Braga (1932–2003), is probably better known for her short stories about small-town Portuguese life and her writings on China and, particularly, Macau, than for her descriptions of Great Britain. Unlike the economic migrants in Lewycka's novels, Braga was educated and relatively independent; she came to Britain not for political or financial reasons, but to perfect her English. She funded her studies at language schools by working as an au pair in Worcester, then Inverness. It was an investment in her future that enabled her to become a teacher of English and a translator in later life, and that gave her the linguistic skills to travel the world.

She describes her experiences and impressions of 'as terras de sua majestade' [Her Majesty's lands] in memoirs, such as her 'autobiografia romanceada' [fiction-

---

[4] Queirós, José Maria Eça de, *Os Maias: episódios da vida romântica* [1888] (Lisbon: Livros do Brasil, 1992).
[5] Luís Amorim de Sousa, *Londres e Companhia* (Lisbon: Assírio e Alvim, 2004).
[6] Maria Velho da Costa, *O Mapa Cor de Rosa* (Lisbon: Dom Quixote, 1984).
[7] Helder Macedo, *Partes de África* (Lisbon: Presença, 1991), *Pedro e Paula* (Lisbon: Presença, 1998), *Vícios e Virtudes* (Lisbon: Presença, 2000) and *Sem Nome* (Lisbon: Presença, 2005).

alized autobiography] *Estátua de Sal* (1969),[8] and also through her fiction, in short stories like 'Estação Morta' and 'Os Rostos de Jano'.[9] Her characters, especially the women, feel a restlessness and a need to escape from convention and routine that often impels them to travel abroad. They thereby gain not only an outsider's perspective of the new territory, but also a different attitude towards 'home'; hence the title *Estátua de Sal* [pillar (literally statue) of salt], which alludes to the consequences of looking back (although her home city of Braga is hardly Sodom or Gomorrah). In a city full of ancient churches, the writer grew up hearing stories and seeing photos of relatives who had emigrated to Brazil or travelled through Europe, some of whom made their fortunes abroad, others returning unsuccessful and humiliated.[10] She was lucky enough to have her family's support and, being an unmarried orphan, did not need a father's or husband's permission to travel abroad.

For a woman of that time, in Salazar's Portugal, her travels were extraordinary. She worked at convent schools in various major cities of the disintegrating empire, starting in Angola in 1961, from where she was evacuated to Goa, shortly before *that* territory was, in turn, reclaimed forcibly by India. She was then moved to Macau, which was still firmly under Portuguese administration, and stayed there for three years, starting to write her semi-autobiographical *crónicas* and short stories during this last period. Macau seems to be the place with which she found most affinity: the site of multiple languages and identities, neither totally Chinese nor totally Portuguese, neither completely ancient nor thoroughly modern, but fluctuating somewhere in-between. The experience is intense and she intends to capture every emotional moment, as she states on the very first page of *Estátua de Sal*: 'Ando a viver esta ponta de Portugal na China com tal perscrutação e sentimento como alguém a fazer exame de consciência na véspera de morrer' [I am living and experiencing this speck of Portugal in China with as much attention and intensity as someone on their deathbed examining their conscience].[11] She returned to Lisbon in 1965 and was careful not to comment on the political situation in Portugal until after the 1974 revolution, so she was not in self-imposed exile against the regime, although she did not approve of it.

The importance of having access to an intimate, personal space (what we might call 'a room of her own') wherever she travelled, was paramount and she recreated in her works numerous rooms where she dwelt, and the views from them. In her texts she invests the objects that surround her, particularly those that always accompany her on her travels, such as certain books, with intense symbolic meaning, including Camilo's *Novelas do Minho*, whose caricatures of

---

[8] Maria Ondina Braga, *Estátua de Sal*, edição refundida e ampliada (Lisbon: Círculo de Leitores, 1976).

[9] These are the title stories in two collections: *Estação Morta* (Lisbon: Vega, 1980) and *Os Rostos de Jano* (Lisbon: Bertrand, 1973).

[10] For example, in *Estátua de Sal*, p. 97, or the story 'O Tio Joaquim', in *A Revolta das Palavras* (Lisbon: Bertrand, 1975), pp. 49–54.

[11] Braga, *Estátua de Sal*, p. 5. All translations from Portuguese are my own.

'morgadas velhas' [old tenant women] always make her laugh. She describes the view from each of her windows, highlighting the frontier between the safe domestic habitat and the potentially dangerous unknown beyond.

She is drawn to places through which many people pass, or where they halt only temporarily, such as waiting rooms,[12] cafés, bars, hotels, airports, markets[13] — spaces where her protagonists can watch unnoticed from the sidelines: 'Sempre achei valer a pena observar as pessoas, imaginar-lhes vidas, fixá-las na memória, ignorando-as' [I have always found it worthwhile to observe people, imagine their lives, fix them in my memory, without knowing them].[14] She is always aloof, even when accompanied, unable to empathize with people or feel totally comfortable in her surroundings.

When staying for some time in one place, Braga describes how she likes to wander through cities in the early morning or late evening, when solitude is guaranteed, but there is always a frisson of danger and the possibility of an unexpected encounter. This experience of being in motion or in transit is key to the way she constructs her identity because it emphasizes the journey rather than the arrival and allows the traveller to wallow in anticipation and dreams that are never quite fulfilled by the reality of reaching the destination: 'A única pena era saber que tinha de chegar. Imaginava-me a seguir nesse comboio louco (serpente de lenda) sempre, sempre [...]. Fechava os olhos em cada estação, como num sonho de que não se deseja acordar, atado pelos fios do subconsciente' [The one thing that spoiled it was knowing that I had to arrive. I would imagine myself staying on that crazy train (legendary serpent) for ever and ever [...]. I would close my eyes at each station, as if in a dream from which one never wants to wake, tied by the threads of the subconscious].[15] Reflecting on another voyage, Braga again emphasizes journey rather than arrival, as can be seen in the epigrammatic phrase: 'Partir é esperança. Chegar desencanto' [Leaving is expectation. Arriving, disappointment].[16]

The dissatisfaction and melancholy of her writing links in with her narrators' and characters' tendency to flirt with others but draw back before too much intimacy is reached. She rarely speaks of the difficulties of being away from home but allows her nostalgia and yearning to show through by her constant references to Braga and Portugal, woven between her excited impressions of newly-discovered lands. In fact, she claims not to feel *saudades* for any place she has lived in, although her insistence upon revisiting those places through her writing would seem to contradict such a statement. She writes about them in retrospect, in diary format (*Estátua de Sal*), as reportage (*Passagem do Cabo*),[17] and

---

[12] Braga, 'Salas de Espera', in *A Revolta das Palavras*, pp. 89–91.
[13] Braga, 'Mercados', in *A Revolta das Palavras*, pp. 105–07.
[14] Braga, *Estátua de Sal*, p. 125.
[15] Braga, *Estátua de Sal*, p. 14.
[16] Braga, *Estátua de Sal*, p. 79.
[17] Braga, *Passagem do Cabo* (Lisbon: Caminho, 1994).

in fiction (*Nocturno em Macau*).[18] This looking back from the present enables her to make comparisons between Portugal, Britain, Angola and Macau, in relation to any number of events or sights that have particularly impressed her: rainstorms, Easter celebrations, markets, Autumn, the habit of taking tea. She may conclude that she prefers one example, but usually she finds pleasure in each, satisfied at having witnessed such a variety of alternatives. Thus 'Sonhar com lagartos em Angola traz-me a infância em Braga' [Dreaming of lizards in Angola brings back my childhood in Braga],[19] or 'Dias assim [de cacimbo, em Angola], que crescem devagar entre o cinzento e o lilás, e que me lembram os de Londres, embora sem frio nem chuvisco' [Stormy days like this, that grow slowly between grey and lilac, and that remind me of the ones in London, although without the cold and the drizzle].[20]

Braga in Britain: Non-Fictional Writing

Braga had lived in Britain in the mid-1950s. Her perception of the country was heavily influenced by what she had read before venturing there: from fairy tales,[21] to Dickens, Robert Louis Stevenson and the Brontës. Her enthusiasm and wide-eyed curiosity pervade her words, despite the early clumsiness she felt as 'quem, vindo de muito longe, se não habituou ainda à realidade que o cerca' [someone who, coming from a long way away, had not yet got used to the reality around them].[22] Her experiences were, in the main, positive, and it was here that she learned how to observe and absorb the sights and impressions of a foreign culture:

> Cada manhã, nova confiança, novo incentivo vinham ao meu encontro no escovar dos cabelos, no enrolar da trança, no engolir do chá fumegante ao pequeno-almoço [...]. Comecei a reparar melhor na riqueza de formas imaginosas nas montras de pastelaria, e a descobrir mistérios, talvez de mais ninguém pressentidos, na majestade sombria de S. James Palace, no movimento das ruas, no contorno das estátuas.[23]

---

[18] Braga, *Nocturno em Macau* (Lisbon: Caminho, 1991).
[19] Braga, *Passagem do Cabo*, p. 18.
[20] Braga, *Passagem do Cabo*, p. 41. The English weather depresses her on other occasions too, and she reflects how it has influenced the character of the natives: 'Na época em que vivi em Inglaterra, década de cinquenta, era o chuvisco, ping-ping, meses seguidos, uma morrinha, uma melancolia. Quase todo o ano Inverno, lá [...]. Uma humidade que o espesso nevoeiro ia peneirando e nos penetrava. Assim pela Primavera adiante. A Primavera dos piqueniques pelos prados com termos de chá e gabardina pela cabeça. Que enquanto nós tínhamos connosco a fé, os ingleses tinham a fleuma' [The time when I lived in England, in the fifties, it was showers, ping-ping, months on end, a light drizzle, a melancholia. Winter almost all year round, there. A damp that filtered through the thick fog and penetrated us. Like that from spring onwards. Spring of picnics on the meadows with flasks of tea and mackintoshes over our heads. Whereas we had our faith, the English had their reserve]. *Passagem do Cabo*, p. 36.
[21] Braga, *Estátua de Sal*, p. 18.
[22] Braga, *Estátua de Sal*, p. 70.
[23] Braga, *Estátua de Sal*, p. 11.

[Every morning, a new confidence, a new sense of purpose came to me as I was brushing my hair, tying up my plait, swallowing down steaming tea at breakfast [...]. I started to take more notice of the richness of the imaginative shapes in the cake-shop displays, and discover mysteries, maybe unsuspected by anybody else, in the dark majesty of St James's Palace, in the movement in the streets, in the contours of the statues.]

It is a difficult task, not without sacrifice and pain, but its rewards are priceless:

> E eu, milagrosamente, nesse labirinto de vidas, nesse mundo pesado de civilização e sofisma, velho de tudo ter experimentado e consumido, eu a encontrar a semente pura da existência! Precisara, sem dúvida, de cavar o monte de esterco com as próprias unhas. Fora-me exigido um grande, um penoso esforço, e uma vontade de homem. [...]. Mas, ao fim de um ano [...], pude contemplar na palma da mão o verdadeiro tesouro. Não era felicidade, alegria, compreensão. Era mais. Laivado da angústia das horas e do desconsolo de mim mesma, era algo imenso, poderoso, inexplicável: a vida![24]

> [And I, miraculously, in that maze of lives, in that world heavy with civilization and sophism, old from having experienced and consumed everything, I was finding the pure seed of existence! I had needed, it was true, to scrape through the mound of dung with my own nails. A great, a painful effort was demanded of me, and a man's will. [...]. But, at the end of a year [...], I was able to contemplate the real treasure in the palm of my hand. It was not happiness, joy, understanding. It was something more. Marked with the anguish of hours and my distress, it was something immense, powerful, inexplicable: life!]

Life itself is her subject, then. She watches and then describes the sights and sounds of the streets, the shops, the parks and the passers-by of all kinds:

> Gente de todas as idades, de todas as condições, de todas as raças, em Hyde Park, nesta tarde anunciadora de Primavera. Senhoras, homens, crianças, ingleses. Vagabundos de cabelo ao vento. Marinheiros de andar gingado e olhar livre. Indianos. Negros. Chineses. Cavalos. Pássaros. Carneiros. Mas eu só encontro árvores — árvores idosas, quietas, graves, árvores a cujo tronco seria bom encostar a cabeça e chorar.[25]

> [People of all ages, all conditions, all races, in Hyde Park, on that afternoon heralding Spring. Women, men, children, English people. Tramps with bare heads. Sailors with a rolling gait and roaming gaze. Indians. Blacks. Chinese. Horses. Birds. Lambs. But I only encounter trees — trees that are aged, still, serious, trees upon whose trunk it would be good to rest my head and cry].

The city swallows up ('engolia') pedestrians and closes its doors to outsiders: 'Londres estava toda de portas adentro' [the whole of London was indoors].[26] It is dark, wet and threatening, especially in the half-light of dusk, when 'os anúncios luminosos [...] punham-me na alma frémitos indefiníveis' [the illuminated

---

[24] Braga, *Estátua de Sal*, pp. 11–12.
[25] Braga, *Estátua de Sal*, p. 13.
[26] Braga, *Estátua de Sal*, p. 16.

signs [...] filled my soul with indefinable shivers].[27] In contrast, the quiet street in Worcester where she lodges, suddenly illuminated by moonlight, is 'envergonhada, como mulher surpreendida nua' [embarrassed, like a woman caught naked].[28] But being the *flâneur*, stranger or observer is not a comfortable position, for it implies isolation and distance from human contact. The busy streets of London at dusk are where Braga felt most strongly 'as unhas venenosas da solidão' [the poisonous claws of loneliness].

Nature is not threatening; on the contrary, it fascinates her, especially flowers (daffodils, honeysuckle, lilies), the weather and the changing seasons, which inspire pastoral idylls:

> Primavera! [...] Na Inglaterra: o campo! Não há outro tempo lindo naquele país sombroso. Ficam os prados de veludo e de malmequeres amarelos como topázios a brilhar ao sol — o sol que, surgindo após três meses de ausência, deixa os ingleses estonteados. [...]. Ao pé do Tamisa, que, passando Oxford, aliviado da sua gravidade Londrina, é todo claro e leve como um turista, as vacas gordas, belas, no pastio, têm imponência de deusas.[29]

> [Spring! [...] In England: the countryside! There's no time as lovely in that gloomy country. The meadows turn to velvet and yellow daisies like topazes shining in the sun — the sun which, coming out after three months of absence, leaves the English stunned. [...]. Beside the Thames, which, after Oxford, relieved of its London severity, is as clear and light as a tourist, the fat, beautiful cows in the pasture are as impressive as goddesses].

Braga conjures up subtle portraits of the most memorable members of the families with whom she lodged, the décor of their houses, their lives, routines and customs, from breakfasts to church fêtes, and celebrations at Christmas, Easter and Lent. Incarnations of these characters, exotic to the contemporary Portuguese readership, and maybe to a modern British public, are also transported into her fiction. Mr Green, for example, protagonist of the eponymous short story 'O Homem-Pássaro', meets the narrator on a cargo-boat travelling between Singapore and Sri Lanka. Her tone is almost that of a pensive anthropologist, showing considerable detachment when describing people, and little affection. The children she cares for will grow up to be 'os comedidos, os fleugmáticos [*sic*] cidadãos britânicos do futuro' [the reserved, phlegmatic British citizens of the future].[30] Her hosts have their habits and foibles: Mrs Mills, 'altamente

---

[27] Braga, *Estátua de Sal*, p. 18. Later in the book she describes 'a hora dos pobres' on winter mornings in London, and the people who inhabit the streets at that time: newspaper-sellers, street-sweepers, snow-clearers, p. 59.
[28] 'Da janela da sala, ao fim da tarde, a cidade de tijolo e lousa, envolta no fumo das chaminés e na neblina do rio, tinha a tonalidade roxa das elegias e fazia pensar nas histórias da infância: a Silvaninha Presa e o Barba Azul...' [From the living-room window, in the evening, the city of brick and slate, enveloped in the smoke from the chimneys and the mist from the river, had the purplish tinge of elegies and reminded me of the stories from my childhood: the Silvaninha Presa [a maiden imprisoned, Rapunzel-like] and Bluebeard], Braga, *Estátua de Sal*, p. 18.
[29] Braga, *Estátua de Sal*, p. 9.
[30] Braga, *Estátua de Sal*, p. 60.

objectiva e prática' [highly objective and practical],[31] the house-proud doctor's wife in Worcester, and the Reverend Knowles, Dean of Inverness Cathedral, who reads *Punch*, serves the vegetables at the dinner table like a good patriarch, and takes his family caravanning.[32] With the kindly Knowles family, the young Braga feels comfortable and almost happy 'facto, antes, raro comigo' [something that before then hardly ever happened]. Interestingly, the contentment she finds by the fireside in Inverness is described mournfully in terms of lack of movement and lack of consciousness: 'Algo semelhante a não saber nada nem ter desejos. Quase como dormir' [Like knowing nothing and wanting nothing. Almost like sleeping].[33] Braga remembers objects and spaces that gave her particular pleasure or satisfaction: the playroom in Worcester, 'a sala mais modesta e despersonalizada da casa [...] onde tudo parecia estar por engano e envergonhado' [the most modest and depersonalized room in the house [...] where everything seemed to be there by mistake and seemed ashamed] is the only room in the house 'onde me era possível encontrar-me' [where I could find myself].[34]

Back Home: Recounting Emigrant Experiences

In other stories, Portuguese characters return home after long journeys and answer relatives' questions about life in England. In 'Lua de Sangue', Inês Carvalho travels back to northern Portugal after three years of studying in England to live with her sick grandfather. Home means familiarity, hearing her surname pronounced correctly, different responsibilities, no cleaning. The new maid is shocked to hear that her mistress did the housework in her lodgings in England.[35] Cousin Justina mixes enquiries about 'abroad' with news from home:

> E como era a tua vida em Inglaterra, Inesinha? [...]. Bem... olhava por crianças. Olhava por crianças e estudava. Ah, sim? [...] E que falasse um bocadinho inglês, um bocadinho, só, para ela ouvir. Como se diz, por exemplo, 'obrigada' em inglês? [...]. *Thank you, thank you so much*. Prima era *cousin*. A outra abanava a cabeça. Ai minha filha, como é que te avinhas por lá com a embrulhada dessa língua?'[36]

---

[31] Braga, *Estátua de Sal*, p. 70.

[32] Braga joins the family on a caravanning trip, and the excitement of eating and sleeping outdoors, not to mention the knobbly knees and kilts of the 'escoceses altos e velhos' [tall elderly Scots], is almost reminiscent of the adventures of Enid Blyton's characters, *Estátua de Sal*, pp. 38, 39.

[33] Braga, *Estátua de Sal*, p. 41.

[34] Braga, *Estátua de Sal*, p. 31.

[35] 'Um turbilhão, a Mrs Jackson. [...] E as limpezas semanais. Trás-trás, almofadas, a moínha das almofadas. E as carpetes, e as cortinas, e os colchões. Espaçoso como uma igreja, o *hall*. Uma jibóia com uma concha na cauda, o aspirador' [A whirlwind, Mrs Jackson. [...] And the weekly clean. Bang bang, cushions, beating the cushions. And the rugs, and the curtains, and the mattresses. As spacious as a church, the hall. A snake, with a shell over its tail, the vacuum cleaner], Braga, 'Lua de Sangue', in *Lua de Sangue* (Lisbon: Rolim, 1986), pp. 123–70 (p. 124).

[36] Braga, 'Lua de Sangue', p. 126. Braga experienced the opposite when living in Worcester and her young charges wanted to hear her speaking Portuguese. She recited the poem 'A

[So how was your life in England, Inês, dear? [...]. Well, I looked after children. I looked after children and studied. Oh, did you? [...]. And could she speak a bit of English, just a bit, just to hear it. How do you say 'thank you' for example, in English? [...]. *Thank you, thank you so much*. Cousin was *cousin*. The other one shook her head. Oh, my dear, how did you manage over there with that muddle of a language?]

To her grandfather's question as to whether she was happy in England, Inês replies 'Gostei, e vi-me grega também' [I enjoyed it, and was confused by it too].[37] Her ambivalent feelings about the experience are smoothed over just through the action of explaining: 'à medida que lhe contava, tudo se ia tornando menos importante do que lá se lhe afigurava, e também menos terrível. Uma libertação?' [as she told him about it, everything started becoming less important than it had seemed to her there, and less awful too. A liberation?].[38] Not only has being in England meant hardship and hard work, the fact that she got through it and can actually describe it helps her appreciate her achievement.

All the characters who cross the Channel seem to go through a rite of passage in Great Britain, whether through falling in love, or gaining work experience, or simply meeting people who change their lives. Mme Henriette, the hotel manageress in the story 'Estação Morta' represents the invisible immigrant worker. She finds a job as a maid in Brighton, working for a family who assume that her name is Maria ('É Maria, não é? Vocês lá são todas Marias' [It's Maria, isn't it? You are all Marias over there].[39] Maria Henriqueta Pires Salvado ('filha de pequenos burgueses e viúva de um amanuense' [the daughter of petit-bourgeois parents and widow of an amanuensis]) is submitted to the indignity of being taught a little English by and having to obtain a reference from a Portuguese woman who used to be in her own family's employ. A middle-class immigrant, she feels excluded by the English and her *conterrâneos* [fellow countrymen or women] abroad alike, describing herself forlornly as a *mestiça* [half-breed]: 'Olhe, das portuguesas que encontrei nesse país nenhuma foi boa para mim. Eu não era propriamente do povo, como as demais emigrantes, raras à data, nem tão-pouco rica. Uma espécie de mestiça, desdenhada de ambas as partes' [You see, of all the Portuguese women I met in that country none was kind to me. I wasn't really working class, like the other emigrants, few at that time, nor was I rich. A kind of half-breed, rejected by both sides].[40]

Nau Catrineta' and told them about the Portuguese voyages of exploration to India, 'E os mocinhos muito atentos e de olhos arregalados. E ao fim, escangalhados de riso. Goodness! Então o Português assim uma toada, al-al-al, assim uma cantilena?' [And the children were very attentive, with their eyes round in wonder. And at the end, they split their sides laughing. Goodness! So Portuguese sounds like that, al-al-al, like a chant?], in *Passagem do Cabo*, p. 91.
[37] Braga, 'Lua de Sangue', p. 129.
[38] Braga, 'Lua de Sangue', p. 132.
[39] Braga, 'Estação Morta', p. 46.
[40] Braga, 'Estação Morta', p. 47.

The one job Mme Henriette does find satisfying is working as a lady's companion (to 'Lady Hamilton') in Wales, where both women work on the farm during the war effort. It is in Lady Hamilton's 'castelo' [castle] that she acquires the skills necessary to open a small hotel, which she proceeds to do, first in Bath, then in London, and then on her eventual return to Portugal. Her reminiscences of the time she has spent in Britain, confided to the narrator, make up a considerable interlude in the text about the Portuguese hotel during the off season, offering a counterpoint to the latter's own story of rootlessness and self-exile.

The short story collection *Os Rostos de Jano* features unconventional women who, when faced with a choice, take the most difficult or socially unacceptable one. Cristina, the female protagonist of the eponymous story,[41] also works as a lady's companion, this time in Devon, and she meets fellow countryman Pedro at a church fête in Cornwall where his band made up of immigrant musicians of various nationalities is playing. The figure of Janus in this story represents Pedro's propensity to guilt and fixation on the past, in contrast to his wife Cristina, who always thinks of the present and soon leaves him for Karl, her ex-lover, the ugly yet animally attractive handyman who worked at the house in Devon. It also symbolizes the lack of compatibility between husband and wife: 'Rostos opostos? Sim, mas inseparáveis [...]. Os olhares deles nunca se encontravam' [Opposing faces? Yes, but inseparable [...]. Their gazes never met].[42] They disagree on so many things that the reader understands why their relationship did not succeed.

The narrative passes through Pedro's consciousness and, briefly, Cristina's, yet dwells most on the man's dependent love and his inability to accept rejection. The setting is the flat in Lisbon the couple had shared after they got married. Once 'o lugar onde [...] fora feliz' [the place where he had been happy],[43] it has been closed and 'fúnebre' [funereal] since their separation, symbolizing the death of their relationship: 'Dantes, a casa limpa, arrumada, os móveis a brilhar, o relógio de pesos a marcar solenemente o tempo. Agora, silêncio, pó e sombras' [Previously, the house was clean, tidy, the furniture sparkling, the grandfather clock solemnly marking time. Now, silence, dust and shadows].[44]

Much of the story is told in flashbacks to that time, as Pedro sits in the flat, waiting for Cristina to come and remove her belongings, every item reminding him of her, and their time there together. The atmosphere somehow recalls his grandmother's house, where he used to play with a bronze bust of Janus: 'em criança, representava para mim o centro do mundo. Verde como as plantas, e com um rosto enfrentando as auroras e outro os poentes' [when I was a child, he was the centre of my world. Green like the plants, with one face looking towards the dawns and the other the sunsets].[45] When he inherited the bust, Cristina

---

[41] Braga, *Os Rostos de Jano* (Lisbon: Bertrand, 1973), pp. 135–60.
[42] Braga, 'Os Rostos de Jano', p. 159.
[43] Braga, 'Os Rostos de Jano', 137.
[44] Braga, 'Os Rostos de Jano', 135.
[45] Braga, 'Os Rostos de Jano', 138.

banished it to the utility room, because it was 'agoirento' [a bad omen]. As they drifted apart, Pedro spent more and more time looking at the bust, thinking that it represented not only the present, but also war. And during their last, painful conversation, he realizes that it also encapsulates her attitude to their relationship: 'O presente nunca existiu para ti. Só o passado com Karl... e o futuro à espera dele. Jano! Duas caras! Por isso o detestavas. A tua própria imagem!' [The present never existed for you. Only the past with Karl... and the future waiting for him. Janus! Two faces! That's why you hated him. Your own image!][46]

Pedro's move to London was provoked by his guilt at not supporting an imprisoned colleague for fear of losing his own job. Once there, though, 'Chegara a lavar pratos, a servir à mesa. O curso superior de nada lhe valia — não sabia a língua' [He ended up washing dishes, waiting at table. His degree was worthless to him — he didn't speak the language].[47] When he first meets Cristina, at a very English church fête in Devon, he can tell that she is not English and falls for her 'quase imediatamente' [almost straight away]. She is overjoyed to meet another Portuguese and mistakes her feeling of joy for love, especially because Karl has abandoned her. Pedro cannot wait to tell his English lover, Ann, who spoils him, makes sacrifices for him, dresses up for him, spends the night with him and is clearly in love with him. It is interesting that Cristina leaves her husband for a German, who is described as 'inteligente e com certa cultura' [intelligent and with a certain amount of culture], as if making a definitive move away from her homeland, whereas Pedro chose a fellow Portuguese in preference to his English lover. Only in retrospect does he reconsider: 'Ann era mais bonita e melhor' [Ann was prettier and nicer].[48] They were not social equals, however, even if she was an example to him of stoicism and acceptance:

> Ann, criada de mesa de um restaurante no West End, de poucas letras e sotaque *cockney*, conhecia o amor puro, o amor que tomava principalmente em conta o bem do companheiro. Ann era um livro. Com ela tinha aprendido a estar ali, sem ciúmes nem rancores, diante da mulher que amava e que o ia abandonar.[49]

> [Ann, waitress at a restaurant in the West End, not much education and a Cockney accent, knew pure love, love that puts above all the wellbeing of one's companion. Ann was a book. From her he had learned to be there, without jealousy or rancour, in front of the woman he loved and who was going to leave him].

It is almost as if by creating these characters Braga is suggesting that Portuguese

---

[46] Braga, 'Os Rostos de Jano', 150.
[47] Braga, 'Os Rostos de Jano', pp. 140–41. Ironically, it is Pedro's former workmate, Vítor, who has been in prison for ten years, that represents the future in this story. He is an idealist, the most optimistic person Pedro has met, even after imprisonment under the regime, pp. 154–55.
[48] Braga, 'Os Rostos de Jano', p. 148.
[49] Braga, 'Os Rostos de Jano', p. 151.

women are more adventurous and outward looking, and that Portuguese men cling to them as a link with home, and the promise of a return to Portugal, sooner or later. Cristina changes through her relationship with Karl: 'Entrou de apreciar a espontaneidade agreste de Karl. Gente diferente. Outra raça. Outra educação. Ela é que era preconceituosa e atrasada' [She came to appreciate Karl's rough spontaneity. Different people. Another race. Another background. She was the one who was prejudiced and backward].[50] When she meets Karl years later, after having married Pedro, she is torn. Like Janus, once again, she must choose between heart and head, 'impulso' [compulsion] and 'calmo afecto' [calm affection], Karl and Pedro.

The story focuses on Pedro's attempts to understand why he has been abandoned, whether he should have stayed with Ann, who treated him much better, and how the relationship would have developed if he and Cristina had met under different circumstances, in other words, if they had met in Portugal. In the end, he cannot bear it any longer and runs away from the flat, leaving Cristina there alone. She is much more sanguine and businesslike about their relationship: 'Um contrato de vida em comum durava enquanto essa vida fosse agradável para ambos. Deixara de o ser para ela. Terminara o contrato' [A contract between two people lasted as long as their life together brought pleasure to both. It had stopped doing so for her. She had terminated the contract].[51] Traditional gender roles seem to be reversed in Braga's fiction: the women take the initiative, the men have to deal with the consequences. Women are also more willing to get involved with men from other countries and change their destinies, rather than always intending to return to the homeland.

To conclude, unlike her memoirs, which linger on descriptions of her hosts, Braga's fictional work foregrounds the emigrant experience whereby immigrants try to bond with their fellow countrymen and women in the face of xenophobia and suspicion in the receptor country. Braga's Britain, then, is a composite of largely positive, if occasionally confusing, personal experiences, and more negative experiences lived out by her characters. As more and more Portuguese communities spring up in contemporary Britain and Ireland, it will be interesting to see if, like Lewycka's Ukrainians, they come to play a more visible role in British and/or Portuguese fiction.

St Peter's College, University of Oxford

---

[50] Braga, 'Os Rostos de Jano', p. 153.
[51] Braga, 'Os Rostos de Jano', 149.

Abstracts

Portuguese Migrant Worker Experiences in Northern Ireland's Market Town Economy
MARTIN EATON

ABSTRACT. Post-millennium Portuguese migrant worker flow has seen Northern Ireland emerge as a focal point. Several thousand migrants have been recruited by employment agencies to work in the regions' agricultural harvesting/food processing industries. This article outlines experiences of key migration players in the market towns of Dungannon and Portadown. Analysis shows the Portuguese worker has had significant impact in supplementing and segmenting the local labour market. Problems have emerged and communities have belatedly responded; some attempt has been made to integrate these workers more closely into work and social arenas. However, it is argued that this is a slow process and many Portuguese in Northern Ireland remain in a state of flux.
KEYWORDS. Migrant workers, Northern Ireland, employment agencies, local labour market, flux

RESUMO. A seguir à passagem do milénio, a emigração portuguesa viu surgir a Irlanda do Norte como um novo ponto focal de destino. Vários milhares de emigrantes foram recrutados, através de agências de emprego, para trabalhar na agro-indústria local, nomeadamente na apanha e processamento de produtos alimentares. Este artigo procura analisar o papel importante que estes fluxos migratórios tiveram em alguns mercados regionais, como Dungannon e Portadown. A análise efectuada mostra claramente que os trabalhadores portugueses tiveram um impacto significativo, quer no fortalecimento quer na segmentação do mercado local de trabalho, levando ao aparecimento de problemas, aos quais as comunidades locais responderam só tardiamente. Como resposta, foram feitas tentativas de integração destes trabalhadores, ao nível social e de emprego. Porém, constata-se que este é um processo moroso e que por isso muitos dos portugueses na Irlanda do Norte continuam numa situação de fluxo temporário.
PALAVRAS CHAVE: Trabalhadores emigrantes, Irlanda do Norte, agências de emprego, mercado local de trabalho, fluxo

Portuguese Migrant Workers in the UK: A Case Study of Thetford, Norfolk
JOSÉ CARLOS PINA ALMEIDA AND DAVID CORKILL

ABSTRACT. The aim of this paper is to investigate migration and settlement processes of Portuguese-speaking migrant workers in the UK, in particular in small towns within a rural or semi-rural environment. Although the Portuguese have settled and worked in the UK since the 1950s and 1960s, only recently has it become an important migration destination for them. Although there were some shared characteristics, the migration flows of the 1990s and early 2000s have differed not only in terms of numbers but also with regard to their post-colonial composition and geographical dispersal. Rather than concentrating in London and the south-east, the new migrants have spread across the UK, with notable concentrations in rural areas such as East Anglia. One such concentration in Thetford, Norfolk is the focus of this study that examines migration motives and practice. In particular, it emphasizes the *multi-national* nature of the Portuguese-speaking community and assesses how these economic migrants coped with unemployment and other challenges, often choosing to migrate to yet another country in order to continue their search for a *better life*.

KEYWORDS. Migration, Portuguese, East Anglia, UK, migrant workers, rural towns

RESUMO. O objectivo deste artigo é investigar os processos de migração e fixação de emigrantes lusófonos no Reino Unido, em particular em pequenas cidades em zonas rurais ou semi-rurais. Se bem que o Reino Unido tenha sido destino de alguns fluxos migratórios anteriores, como nas décadas de 1950 e 1960, só recentemente o país se tornou um destino significativo para os emigrantes portugueses. Apesar de haver algumas características comuns entre estes primeiros fluxos migratórios e os da década de 1990 e primeira metade da década de 2000, estes diferem dos anteriores, não só em termos de números e quantidade mas também quanto à sua composição pós-colonial e à sua dispersão geográfica. Em vez de se concentrarem em Londres e no Sudeste, os emigrantes mais recentes têm-se dispersado por todo o país com concentrações em áreas rurais como a East Anglia. Este estudo diz respeito a uma dessas concentrações — Thetford, Norfolk. Analisamos motivos e processos de migração; sublinhamos a natureza *multi-nacional* da comunidade lusófona; estudamos como esta comunidade reage aos desafios recentes como o desemprego e concluímos que a resposta passa muitas vezes pela decisão de migrar novamente para outro país, na constante procura de *uma vida melhor*.

PALAVRAS CHAVE. Migração portuguesa, East Anglia, Reino Unido, trabalhadores migrantes, zonas rurais

Migrant Identities, Sociolinguistic and Sociocultural Practices: Portuguese and Spanish Migrations to the South Coast of England
JAINE BESWICK AND ALICIA POZO-GUTIÉRREZ

ABSTRACT. This essay presents a research project based around Bournemouth in Dorset, aimed at mapping out and characterizing the mid- and long-term presence of Portuguese-speaking migrants, using Spanish-speaking migrants as a comparative. By adopting an interdisciplinary perspective, we focus on the context of arrival and on migrants' identification patterns, in order to explore the relationship between language use and evolving strategies adopted at different stages of the distinct migratory trajectories. From a longitudinal perspective, these are contextually convergent but theoretically divergent: whilst the socio-economic and sociopolitical migrant contexts share similar background characteristics, their evolution, maintenance and migration dynamics differ considerably.

We propose that these migrations are not necessarily definitive regarding identification strategies, since immersion and long-term projection into the receptor society do not always imply full integration, nor do they always entail ethnic grouping. Rather, the migrants of this study are positioned along a continuum of multiple patterns of accommodation manifest in different sociolinguistic and sociocultural ways.

KEYWORDS. Diaspora, identification strategies, migratory trajectories, integration, ethnic grouping

RESUMO. Este ensaio apresenta um projecto de investigação centrado em Bournemouth, Dorset, destinado a mapear e caracterizar a presença de imigrantes de língua portuguesa a médio e longo prazo, usando como elemento comparativo os imigrantes de língua espanhola. No âmbito de uma perspectiva interdisciplinar, concentrámos a nossa análise no contexto de chegada e nos padrões de identificação dos migrantes, para assim podermos explorar a relação entre o uso da língua e a evolução das estratégias adoptadas em diferentes fases das distintas trajectórias migratórias. Desde uma perspectiva longitudinal, estas trajectórias são contextualmente convergentes mas teoricamente divergentes: enquanto os contextos sócio-económicos e sócio-políticos dos migrantes partilham características semelhantes, a sua evolução, a sua manutenção e a sua dinâmica migratória diferem consideravelmente.

Consideramos que estas migrações não são necessariamente definitivas com respeito a estratégias de identificação, dado que a imersão e a projecção na sociedade receptora a longo prazo nem sempre implicam integração completa, por um lado, ou agrupamento étnico, por outro. Em contrapartida, os migrantes deste estudo situam-se ao longo de uma gama de padrões múltiplos de adaptação à sociedade receptora, expressos em maneiras sociolinguísticas e sócio-culturais diferentes.

PALAVRAS CHAVE. Diáspora, estratégias de identificação, trajectórias de migração, integração, agrupamento étnico

A Transnational Space? Transnational Practices, Place-Based Identity and the Making of 'Home' among Brazilians in Gort, Ireland
OLIVIA SHERINGHAM

ABSTRACT. This essay explores the transnational and place-making practices of Brazilian migrants in the Irish town of Gort in County Galway. Since the first arrival of Brazilian workers in Gort, in 1999, many more arrived to live and work there, with the numbers (although now decreasing) reaching a peak of nearly half the town's population of 3000. Despite some media coverage keen to highlight the novelty of the phenomenon or to expose any potential scandal, very little has been written about the migrants' experiences and their everyday lives. Drawing on empirical research conducted in Gort in 2008, this paper considers the 'transnational spaces' constructed by Brazilian migrants, and examines how such spaces relate to their local, place-based, attachments in the town.

KEYWORDS. Brazilian migrants, Ireland, transnationalism, local attachment, place-based identities

RESUMO. O ensaio analisa as práticas transnacionais e localizadas dos migrantes brasileiros na vila irlandesa de Gort no condado de Galway. Desde a chegada dos primeiros trabalhadores brasileiros em 1999 muitos mais migraram, atingindo o número máximo de 3000, ou seja, metade da população da vila, embora se verifique agora o declínio desse processo de migração. Apesar de alguma cobertura mediática da novidade do fenómeno e de algum escândalo, quase nada foi escrito sobre as experiências dos migrantes e as suas vidas diárias. Baseado em pesquisa empírica conduzida em Gort em 2008, este artigo considera os 'espaços transnacionais' construídos pelos migrantes brasileiros e examina como esses espaços se relacionam com as ligações locais na vila.

PALAVRAS CHAVE. Migrantes brasileiros, Irlanda, transnacionalismo, ligação local, identidades localizadas

Migrant Languages in a Multi-Ethnic Scenario: Brazilian Portuguese-Speakers in London
ANA SOUZA

ABSTRACT. This essay addresses issues of language use and the reciprocal relationship between language and identity in the context of the migration of Portuguese-speakers to London from Brazil. It also underlines the importance of considering varying social factors as well as the influence of migrants' objectives and goals within the receptor society in obtaining a better appreciation of such relationships. My empirical investigation centres upon a group of Brazilian families whose children attend extra-curricular Portuguese language lessons. Through in-depth interviews, I examine the reasons behind the mothers' multiple and changeable self-identification practices manifest through language use, as well as the impact of the importance they attach to their ethnicity on their children's emotional and instrumental links to their community language.

KEYWORDS. Brazilian migration, Portuguese language, mixed-heritage children, migrant mothers, language and identity

RESUMO. O artigo aborda o problema do uso da língua e das relações recíprocas entre língua e identidade no contexto da migração de brasileiros para Londres. O artigo sublinha a importância de se considerarem factores locais a par dos objectivos dos migrantes no seio da sociedade receptora. A pesquisa empírica está centrada num grupo de famílias brasileiras cujas crianças recebem lições extra-curriculares de português. Através de entrevistas aprofundadas, são examinadas as razões subjacentes às práticas linguísticas de auto-identificação múltipla e variável das mães, bem como o impacto da importância atribuída à etnicidade no enquadramento emocional da criança, obtida através da ligação instrumental à comunidade de língua.

PALAVRAS CHAVE. Migração brasileira, língua portuguesa, crianças mistas, mães migrantes, língua e identidade

Family and Transmission: Collective Memory in Identification Practices of Madeirans on Jersey
VANESSA MAR-MOLINERO

ABSTRACT. Over the past sixty years, many Madeirans have migrated to Jersey, the largest of the Channel Islands. The vast majority have been seasonal economic migrants who went there to work either in agriculture or in the service sector. However, and in particular since the entry of Portugal into the EU, many Madeirans have relocated their existing families to the island and appear to have settled on a long-term basis. Others have started families on the island. This essay presents my on-going research into the familial transmission of memory. My investigations centre on the children of such migrants and focuses on the extent to which their families, their family lives, their upbringing and their community have, through collective memory, affected, shaped, created or recreated their ethnic, social, cultural and linguistic identification practices.

KEYWORDS. Collective memory, identification practices, identities, community

RESUMO. Nos últimos sessenta anos, muitos Madeirenses migraram para Jersey, a maior das Ilhas do Canal. A grande maioria foram migrantes económicos sazonais, e foram lá para trabalhar nos sectores de agricultura ou de serviços. No entanto, e em especial desde a entrada de Portugal na UE, muitos Madeirenses deslocaram as suas famílias para a ilha e parecem ter resolvido ficar fora de Madeira de longo prazo. Para outros, os seus filhos nasceram mesmo na ilha. Este ensaio apresenta a minha investigação em curso sobre a

transmissão familiar de memória. As minhas investigações concentram-se em os filhos dos migrantes e em a medida em que através da memória colectiva, as suas famílias, a sua vida familiar, a sua educação e as suas comunidades, tivessem afectado, moldado, criado ou recriado a suas práticas de identificação étnica, social, cultural e linguística.
PALAVRAS CHAVE. Memória colectiva, práticas de identificação, identidades, comunidade

Nas Terras de Sua Majestade: Portuguese Emigrants to Britain in the Works of Maria Ondina Braga
CLAIRE WILLIAMS

ABSTRACT. The Portuguese have been emigrating around the globe for centuries, and the number of emigrant communities in the UK has grown substantially over the twentieth century, and into the twenty-first. Despite this fact, however, both literary accounts of life in 'as terras de sua majestade' and modern travel writing are few and far between. Maria Ondina Braga's depiction of Britain in the 1950s, in her fictionalised autobiography and also her fiction, captures not only the culture clash, but vividly portrays middle-class households with charm and perspicacity. This essay considers how she constructs her outsider's view of Britain and the British, and how crossing the channel changes the lives of her characters.
KEYWORDS. Portuguese literature, Maria Ondina Braga, Portuguese migration, visions of Britain, autobiography and fiction

RESUMO. Os portugueses emigraram durante séculos para vários pontos do globo, mas só nas últimas décadas do século XX e no início do século XXI começaram a tomar como destino o Reino Unido em número significativo. Apesar deste fenómeno, as narrativas de vida 'em terras de sua majestade' e as narrativas de viagem são escassas. A descrição da Grã-Bretanha por Maria Ondina Braga nos anos de 1950, na sua autobiografia ficcionalizada e na sua ficção, captura o choque cultural, enquanto nos dá um retrato vivo de casas de classe média com encanto e perspicácia. Este ensaio considera o processo de construção pela autora do ponto de vista do estrangeiro da Grã-Bretanha e dos britânicos, bem como o papel fundamental da travessia do Canal na mudança de vida dos seus personagens.
PALAVRAS CHAVE. Literatura portuguesa, Maria Ondina Braga, migração portuguesa, visões da Grã-Bretanha, autobiografia e ficção